The Creative Director:

Alternative  WITHDRAWN

Rehearsal

Techniques

by

Edward S. Lisk

Director of Bands, Music Supervisor
Oswego City School District
Oswego, New York

The Creative Director: Alternative Rehearsal Techniques

Library of Congress Catalog Card Number: 87-90906
Copyright Registration: TX 2 078 725
ISBN: 0 - 9624308 - 0 - 3

First Edition..........March 1987
Second Edition......September 1990
Third Edition.........March 1991

Printed in the United States of America

MEREDITH MUSIC PUBLICATIONS

*****

In loving memory of my daughter,

Janice Theresa Lisk

September 20, 1957 - February 5, 1982

*****

To
My wife,

Dorie

My daughters,

Carol Anne
Jean Marie

My mother and father,

Jennie and Edward A. Lisk

"With all my love and heartfelt appreciation."

*****

Acknowledgments

✳✳✳✳✳✳✳✳✳

This text has taken approximately ten years to complete. I am most humble and appreciative to all those individuals who became a part of this text through their influence, assistance, and support.

My love and appreciation to my loving wife Dorie, and my daughters, Jan, Carol and Jean, for their unending patience and love in accepting, understanding, encouraging, and supporting my life as a musician/teacher. Dedicating this text in their honor is only a small way I can express my appreciation and love for my wife and our daughters. I hope this book will make them proud.

My love to my beautiful grandchildren; Davey, Emily, and Brian.

To my mother and father, my sister and her family....Thank you for your love and constant support.

My admiration and appreciation to all the Oswego High School Wind Ensemble members without whom I could not have had the inspiration to write this book.

My appreciation to my instrumental staff who supported me in the development of this text; *Anthony Joseph, William Crist, Michael Dunsmoor, Tom Quirk, Steve Landgren, and Rudd Trowbridge.*

To my most *distinguished teacher, advisor and gentleman, Dr. Harwood Simmons.* Dr. Simmons was most influential in my career and studies at Syracuse University School of Music.

To *Joe Riposo*, my long time friend and jazz partner who has helped me so much throughout my career.

✳✳✳✳✳✳✳✳✳

Acknowledgments (cont.)

✱✱✱✱✱✱✱✱✱✱

To our long time family friends; *Duke Borden* and his family, and to our very special "Florida" friends *Elmer and Doris Cook.*

To *Jeff Renshaw* for those perpetual discussions in search for answers and new directions in what we do.

During my years at the Oswego City School District, one item remained consistent......*the commitment and support for academic excellence by our board of education and administration.* The privilege of working for, and receiving total support from past superintendents: *Pete Ahern, Darwin Carlson, Ken Lane, and present Superintendent Edward Garno;* and Administrators: *Fred Maxon, Bill Symons, Frank Warren, Carl Palmitesso, Joe Donovan, Bob Stone, Don Goewey, Fran Witkowski, Ed Cariccioli,* and Assistant Superintendent *Bob Perkins;* past high school principal and board member *Anthony Murabito,* and all *board of education* members who consistently gave their full support to our music program during these past twenty years.

To all the wonderful *band parent* members I had the privilege of working with during these past years. They made it possible for all the students since 1970 to see and experience the United States through musical excellence ! What beautiful memories !

I have been extremely fortunate during my career to have served on adjudication panels with so many *distinguished college and high school band directors throughout the United States. These associations and friendships have instilled a deep appreciation and commitment to my profession.* It is only through these clinician assignments with such distinguished directors that an "instrumental education" is made complete !

For those who have either attended my clinic presentations, or are reading this book for the first time in search of new methods, I sincerely hope that the concepts and techniques will make a small contribution to your programs excellence.

✱✱✱✱✱✱✱✱✱✱

Comments & Reactions:

Excerpt from a review which appeared in the May 1988 issue of "International Journal of Music Education"
"This is a valuable book that encourages band/orchestra directors to look beyond traditional rehearsal procedures and instigate rehearsal structures that foster listening skills through visualization and mental imagery. It will prove valuable in teacher training courses and for student reference as well as for the band/orchestral directors wishing to explore alternative rehearsal techniques. HIGHLY RECOMMENDED."
"I am impressed with the publication and feel that it would be most useful for music educators around the world!"
Gary McPherson., Review Editor - Senior Lecturer....University of New South Wales - Sydney, Australia

****

"Alternative Rehearsal Techniques" offers us the opportunity to teach musical concepts from the *inside*. It develops basic fundamentals through group participation and brings the ensemble experience to the highest level of musical awareness and sensitivity. I enthusiastically recommend this text to all conductors and music educators !"
Anthony J. Maiello, Professor of Music-Director of Bands....George Mason University - Fairfax, Virginia

****

"We have been using *"Alternative Rehearsal Techniques"* with both the middle and upper school bands at Woodward Academy. These techniques have improved the focus of the groups. Individual response is heightened. Warm-up materials used through *Alternative Rehearsal Technique*s prevent common balance, blend and pulse problems found in concert literature."
Marguerite Wilder, Director....Woodward Academy-College Park, Georgia

****

"Our educational system has been criticized for producing students who are not taught to think. *Alternative Rehearsal Techniques* is a solution that offers a systematic approach of practical rehearsal techniques suitable for all committed music educators. This text has been an excellent resource in my teaching as a middle school band director. I have found an approach to teaching music that rewards student and teacher with enthusiastic results. Thank you for an exciting and effective collection of *alternativie rehearsal techniques !"*
William Crist, Middle School Director....Oswego City School District - Oswego, New York

****

"The Creative Director" provides a means to develop instructional techniques which activate the students' thought process and builds mental readiness for music performance. It is highly recommended for those who are interested in the neurological process by which music and music instruction are perceived. This text certainly meets the expectations and needs of our instrumental staff."
Joseph Riposo , Director of Music Education ...Liverpool Central School District - Liverpool, New York

****

"Alternative Rehearsal Techniques" is a systematic plan of teaching combined with learning skills which are easily understood by students and teachers. The learning which takes place eliminates the repetitious quotations that many directors use over and over again to clear up the same problem."
Jack Pinto, Past President....New York State School Music Association

****

"Alternative Rehearsal Techniques" is a must for the director at any level who dares to be imaginative and creative ! This book provides numerous examples of outstanding instructional procedures as well as an unlimited variety of warm-up exercises. I have started re-reading the text for the 3rd time...it has inspired me to become an artistic teacher and conductor !"
John A. Flaver, Elem. Band....Westhill Central Schools, Syracuse, New York

****

"I began using your method after I saw your clinic at the Mid-West. I can't believe the sound my band is getting. I haven't been this excited about rehearsal techniques in a long time. You have a real winner in your publication and I appreciate the incredible amount of time you have spent researching and developing this method. Thanks !!"
Margene Pappas, Middle School Director....Oswego, Illinois

****

"This is the most well constructed method for rehearsal techniques and music instruction I have ever encountered. Very thought provoking, informative and practical !"
1990 Australian National Band Clinic (Western)....Perth, Australia

****

"Alternative Rehearsal Techniques" is truly innovative and has opened my eyes to a "bottomless pit" of ideas and direction. Fantastic and inspiring ! "
1990 Australian National Band Clinic (Eastern)....Sydney, Australia

****

Table of Contents

****

Table of Contents (cont.)

Forward
****

The study of how a person learns is a lifelong quest for teachers. The mere dissemination of information leaves the act of teaching to the students and students find many ways to try to teach themselves, most of them unproductive. When a teacher can direct the learning process into clear and precise channels with time proven methods, the learning is not only faster but results in a higher level of achievement.

This is exactly what Edward Lisk has done for many years with the Oswego Instrumental Music program at Oswego, New York. I have had the privilege of conducting his bands several times and have always been amazed at their superior performance skills. Mr. Lisk has accomplished this through creative study and years of practical application as to how students learn and succeed in musical skills.

He has done this by learning how the brain works, the brain's potential and how to guide this potential. Mr. Lisk has created a scholarly book with practical application, a guide to the understanding of the learning process in instrumental music that is original, a thesis of information that can be found no where else.

I introduce to you a book that will instruct you, that will stimulate your pedagogy and that will open new concepts for your rehearsal techniques.

W. Francis McBeth
Professor of Music - Resident Composer
Ouachita University
Arkadelphia, Arkansas

****

Introduction

✳✳✳✳✳✳✳✳✳✳

The system of rehearsal techniques presented in this method allows the band director to improve rehearsal efficiency through a more effective learning environment with access to the students' fullest musical potential. It provides new concepts, graphic illustrations and instructional procedures designed to enhance and accelerate student performance skills.

The integrated process encourages directors to look beyond conventional rehearsal procedures. Emphasis is placed upon auditory and visual/imagery techniques. Thinking skills and internal pulse are synchronized to assure consistent performance qualities throughout all types of literature demands.

Through this system of musical learning, many problems and inhibitions which may have inadvertently been taught are no longer obstacles to the superior qualities students are capable of achieving. The unique approach opens a "new world" of instructional and rehearsal procedures. As the integrated concepts expand, much of the needless performance and verbal repetition is eliminated. Attention is focused to the control and quality of the student's mental/thinking process. By developing mental readiness or greater concentration within the student, we increase the depth of understanding and produce a more meaningful musical experience. This intense mental focus provides the students with the intrinsic rewards of musical expression. A constant state of attention to performance objectives is assured.

The most exciting aspect of this method is that every student becomes totally involved. It is not a forced, demanded, or dictated teaching technique.

✳✳✳✳✳✳✳✳✳✳

On the following page is a graphic representing the system of musical learning presented in this text. It does not represent a sequential process. The entire foundation is based upon the *Circle of 4ths*. From this point, the director is free to proceed in any direction to acquire the necessary skills for effective musical performance.

An outline for implementing *Alternative Rehearsal Techniques* is found in Chapter 9, page 151.

✳✳✳✳✳✳✳✳✳✳

Integrated Performance Elements

Director determines instructional sequence through:

1. Rehearsal goals and objectives.

2. Literature demands: rhythms, articulation, dynamics, chord qualities, style, balance, blend, etc.

3. Strengths and weakness of band.

4. Short and long range program and performace goals.

Provides unlimited variations to achieve performance objectives.

All ensemble performance skills are placed into a relevant warm-up process.

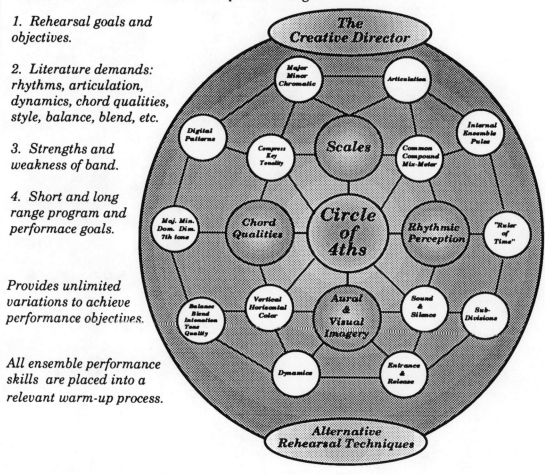

Chapter 1

Rehearsal Structure

Warm-Up

Hemisphericity and Musical Performance

Conflict between Analytical and Wholistic Process

From Mechanical to Artistic Performance

Director Awareness Scale

The beginning of every rehearsal is the most critical area in the development of a superior band program. The traditional term *"warm-up,"* generally implies the physical aspects of performance with brief attention to *mental readiness* for effective rehearsal productivity. Results are minimal if the proper mental preparation of the student is not taken into consideration. Most often we spend the least amount of time in seeking creative approaches to "warm-up," which is the *doorway to success in allowing the students to reach their fullest musical potential.*

The study of learning behavior and the psychology of memory points out that memory for the beginning and end of a rehearsal is almost perfect. The first ten minutes of each rehearsal is the most critical regarding the proportion of information retained. After the first ten minutes, learning drops off rapidly. Studies show that when we are involved in learning, there are four main areas of highest recall: the *BEGINNING,* the *END*, activities *LINKED* to the beginning, and things *OUTSTANDING* (P. Russell, 1979).

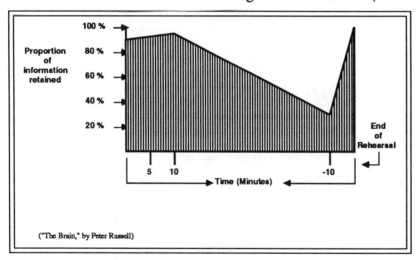

("The Brain," by Peter Russell)

With such information on learning behavior, it is extremely important in how we treat the beginning ten minutes of each rehearsal and what we do after the first ten minutes to eliminate this rapid drop off of concentration. By creating a "Warm-Up" process (first 10 minutes), which is designed to include all musical demands to be addressed during the middle portion of our rehearsal, we can significantly improve student and director performance far beyond the many present but unrelated techniques.

The system of musical learning and performance in this text is designed for the band director to develop rehearsal time more efficiently.

Another area of concern in effective rehearsal structure and techniques is in how we approach *repetition* with students. Repetition is a means of acquiring success to the smallest musical detail. We are aware that any artistic endeavor calls for extraordinary patience with *repetition* to achieve *perfection.* The word "repetition" itself has many implications to students. More often than not, it implies drudgery and consuming inordinate amounts of time. When students are involved with rehearsals that follow identical or habitual patterns each day, drudgery through repetition can create a subconscious negative state and silently stifle the students attitude and ability. *When a person is presented with a sensory signal that is repeated with monotonous regularity, his response to it gradually diminishes until it becomes undetectable. This process is called "habituation." Habituation is a mechanism which keeps the brain from being bothered by continuous unimportant signals* (Bower, 1966).

The prime focus of this text is directed to developing mental readiness and emphasizing auditory skills through creative variations of the "warm-up process." Repetition, *without drudgery or negative reaction,* is easily accomplished through the many methods and techniques in this method. The approach is quite simple. *Never establish a pattern or formula that is habitual. When a habitual pattern in rehearsal structure is formed, the students mental involvement deteriorates.*

To gain a new perspective on our instructional techniques, the following section provides new insights into rehearsal structure and musical performance.

Hemisphericity and Musical Performance

During the past several years, much research has been published pertaining to left and right brain functions. Psychologists, physiologists, and neurologists have found some interesting and pertinent data dealing with how our brain perceives and processes information. Many textbooks have been published with the intent of increasing human potential in a variety of skills and tasks through left and right hemispheric functions.

Throughout my recent study and research in this area, I have found that significant changes can be made to alter and enhance our teaching techniques. *I am not proposing that all teaching techniques be defined and categorized into Left and Right Hemisphere techniques. Scientists involved in this extensive research caution us to its interpretation and application.* However, our study and awareness of Hemisphericity can be of assistance with the questions we may have about student behavior, achievement, and attitude toward musical performance.

Pictured below is a diagram of Left and Right Hemispheric functions. A brief review will allow us to realize some of the activities of the brain during musical performance.

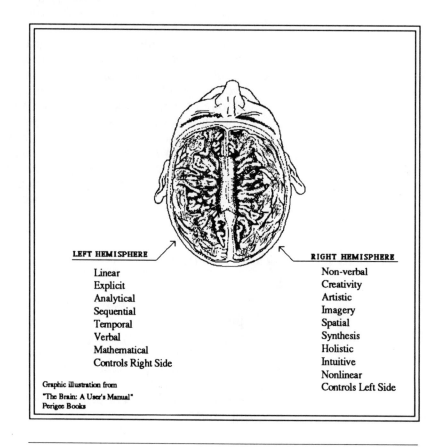

LEFT HEMISPHERE

Linear
Explicit
Analytical
Sequential
Temporal
Verbal
Mathematical
Controls Right Side

RIGHT HEMISPHERE

Non-verbal
Creativity
Artistic
Imagery
Spatial
Synthesis
Holistic
Intuitive
Nonlinear
Controls Left Side

Graphic illustration from
"The Brain: A User's Manual"
Perigee Books

By defining the musical activities and their specializations through left and right brain functions, we can expand our awareness to the unlimited possibilities in rehearsal and teaching procedures.

Left Mode Process

Specifically, the left brain is our logical hemisphere. This side of the brain is involved with language skills. It controls our speech and allows us to read and write. Along with these language skills, the logical and analytical skills required in dealing with mathematical problems are also processed in this side of our brain. It remembers facts, dates, and recalls specifics. Information is processed sequentially or in a step by step manner.

The student who can define, verbally, all aspects of note values, rhythms and sub-divisions, dynamics, meter, scales, chords, keys, fingerings, tempo indications, metronome markings, stylistic terms, composer background, theoretical structure, historical information, etc., is only functioning and processing in an analytical mode.

Rehearsals and lessons devote the greatest portion of time dealing with the correction of notes, key signatures, fingerings, articulation, dynamics, etc., with the teacher monitoring and correcting each detail missed or performed poorly. The student is being conditioned to react to his performance in a negative frame of mind based upon the critical, analytical thought process. Traditional teaching techniques place a premium on the students ability to verbalize such terms and imitate teacher expectations. When an individual can define these terms correctly, it is then assumed a clear understanding has been reached. Upon reaching this technical and verbal ability, the student then proceeds to apply this knowledge to the mechanical demands of the musical instrument. The teacher can also evaluate, by numerical grade, the extent and accuracy of such knowledge.

Such a learning environment conditions the students to consume more time, effort, and attention to the numerical and mechanical results, instead of the "music making" process. Through such emphasis, the "chair position" becomes quite important to the student, rather than the total ensembles ability to perform musically. This condition has been created by the director; it is easy to verify a particular chair position through "scores." Consequently, the program never reaches its fullest potential, because the 3rd clarinet or trumpet section has the "poorest numerical achievers" assigned to the most critical sections. Upper chair players may become disturbed with the performance levels of third chair players. Third chair players are disenchanted in not being able to measure to the expectations of others. A division is created and the entire ensemble never receives or experiences the opportunity to perform as a "whole." There must be time when attention, regardless of the mechanical detail, must focus upon the expressive qualities of the music in a wholistic concept.

Band programs which focus all attention and energy to-ward only left hemispheric activity throughout rehearsals may end up becoming *extremely accurate in the smallest detail, but sterile and methodical in the final performance.* Such results are because the students were deprived of the opportunity to become fully involved in an artistic non-verbal expression. *Phrases and musical statements become mechanically "contrived" in an attempt at projecting some form of expression.*

Left hemispheric activities can be clearly verbalized with a complete understanding and *still* not achieve the real meaning of music! Not until these activities (analytical and wholistic) are processed simultaneously, with the individuals own uniqueness of expressive qualities, can music be made into an expression. This allows the students to project their inner emotions which they sense to the musical composition. The student will experience the true feeling of musical expression and its intensity. The uniqueness of these expressive qualities are determined by the affects and effects of all past experiences involved in forms of learning and living.

Right Mode Process

Specifically, the Right Brain is our intuitive hemisphere. Right brain knowledge is not achieved through words, but through images. It responds to problems wholistically, recognizes faces, understands metaphors, fantasizes, dreams, creates, and imagines. Innate musical talent, as well as the ability to respond to music are right brain functions (although extensive musical education will result in left hemisphere involvement as well). The Limbic System (another part of our brain) is where our emotions emerge from. It is the right hemisphere which is in touch with these feelings.

The quality of the right mode state of consciousness is different from the left mode. The moment of shifting between one mode to the other always remains out of awareness. Once you have made the shift, the difference in the two states is accessible to knowing. The main division is between *Thinking* and *Feeling*.

Most often, because of our educational system, the dominant left always takes over...analyzing, verbalizing, counting, etc. The right allows us to see things which exist in our "minds eye" - visualizing or imagining, recalling things that are real. *Imaging* is a right brain capability. The brain is able to create an image and then "look at it," seeing it as though it is "really there." Research has proven that *by creating strong, vivid images, recall is increased by two and a half times*. Visual images are much better remembered than words. In fact, visual imagery is nearly perfect. *Pictures are sureness and confidence....we don't question our interpretation of a visual experience.*

The ability to activate *musical imagery* is critical in creating an artistic performance. Musical imagery does not necessarily have to be verbally defined, only *activated*. If attempts are made to verbalize, many subtleties will be extinguished or deprived. Techniques of *Activation* are the priority.....*Musical imagery activates a wholistic configuration.*

7

When the teacher is successful in creating, teaching techniques which address both sides (analytical and wholistic), a balance or equilibrium is achieved, allowing the student to make significant improvement with increased personal satisfaction. Thus, a greater interest, motivation for improvement, and a greater sense of value and worth to the discipline of music is realized.

With such knowledge and awareness of Hemisphericity, it is possible to greatly improve teaching techniques to achieve the maximum potential of the band or ensemble. The variations to the rehearsal will quickly sensitize the director and students to the many subtle characteristics of affective learning and appreciation.

Conflict between Analytical (Left) and Wholistic (Right) Process

Conflict between the two thinking processes can create havoc with our intended performance. When such a mental state happens in performance, it suppresses and restricts both the musician and conductor. Whenever we perform in public and mentally revert to an analytical process, the performance becomes quite awkward, clumsy, and lacks flow. The mind is returning to the *analytical-error-detector mode* of *PRACTICE* instead of the *wholistic mind of PERFORMANCE*. When this happens, the performer becomes nervous and attempts to recover.....the mind continues on this analytical-error-detector mode and the result is failure.

The final performance state in which all musicians strive to achieve, when playing or conducting in public, is established throughout many tedious hours of practice. The mind holds a perception regarding the goal of the intended performance and functions in a very analytical process throughout the practice procedure (months, weeks, days), leading to the performance. The closer the performance day, the more the mind functions in a wholistic state, perceiving the composition in *total,* with all segments connected to make musical sense of all the "bits and pieces" worked out through repetitious practice.

This process is similar to golf swing. If the golfer can perceive the complete or "total" swing, his chances are far greater for success. When focusing in on detail such as: *bring the club back slow....left 3 fingers increase pressure on grip....slight pause at the top....swing down....delay wrist release....and at the moment of impact, swing to the outside....* is an extremely conflicting internal procedure which causes physical and mental constraints. Such mechanically contrived mental attention becomes frustrating. The individual never achieves the perceived results in an easy, natural, relaxed flow of motion.

Many instrumental instructional techniques follow the same procedures as outlined with the above golf example. Students, more often than not, experience this mental frustration ending in failure or a lack of desire to proceed because expected outcomes have become hopeless.

From Mechanical to Artistic Performance

I have created a 5 step theory moving from a mechanical to an artistic domain of musical performance (see page 15 for graphic illustration). The intention is to define, in a linear fashion, the various analytical/wholistic procedures involved in developing a musical performance. The 5 levels presented do not happen as specifically defined in a step by step procedure, but are constantly being integrated in the entire process of preparation.

If anything, this theory will allow the band director to view the structure of his/her rehearsal, allowing for modifications and improvement.

Level 1: Analytical, Mathematical, Verbal

The students first experience with a new piece of music deals strictly with a left mode process. All the "mechanics" or mathematical skills necessary in making a series of sounds are processed in an analytical setting, such as time signature, note values, key signature, rhythms, sub-divisions, dynamics, articulation, range, and any complex musical demands which may hamper the skill or finesse of the performance. These signs and symbols are visually scanned and the first attempt is made through sight reading. The prime focus of attention is directed toward analysis of the many "bits and pieces."

Besides the "mechanics" of written notation, attention must also be directed to the physical aspects of making the sound, such as embouchure, hand position, posture and breath support.

Level 2: Repetition

The initial presentation of the musical material in Level 1 allows us to isolate these specifics and practice through *REPETITION*. We consistently stress the need for slow and precise development of the intracacies necessary in achieving an acceptable performance. We achieve correctness by *repetition* of the elements through a logical sequential process.

A part of our brain is called the *cerebellum*. It reacts to this repetition and stores these motor skills. If errors are evident, the cerebellum also stores this incorrect information !! The cerebellum is like our "automatic pilot"; once a series of repetitive actions are done, it assumes we want an automatic reaction to this skill or activity. The most critical concern is that the *cerebellum cannot discern correct from incorrect !!*

Throughout rehearsals, the band director must be extremely cautious about the type of errors being made and how frequently they have occurred. They might have been "built in" through improper practice on the individual students part or the band directors oversight. Without the correctness of the band directors directions, and student understanding, the errors will be a part of the next concert. *The cerebellum would have done its job !*

Level 3: Compositional Structure

As the small details develop and repetition continues, the band director gradually establishes and focuses attention to the "architectural structure" of the musical composition. This is done both on a vertical and horizontal basis with individual students, sections, and total organization. Vertical and horizontal structure occurs simultaneously as attention is directed to accuracy and precision.

Vertically the band must respond to the synchronized reaction of all entrances and releases, visualizing and hearing the total ensemble sound from tuba to piccolo while on a horizontal basis, the sub-divisions must be reacted to in the same synchronized or unified fashion.

The "architectural structure" not only addresses vertical and horizontal sound structure, but also the entire composition. The conductor is shaping the "completeness" and continuity of all musical elements such as phrases, transitions, tempo changes, themes, motif, variations, etc. from beginning to end.

Once these actions become automatic (which is an activity of the cerebellum), and all analytical (left brain) information no longer needs focused attention (similar to driving an automobile), the band is ready for the concert performance.

My experiences lead me to believe that, at this point in performance, a transition is taking place into LEVEL 4.

Level 4: Synthesis, Holistic

When this subtle transition has taken place, we subconsciously make a shift to more right hemispheric functions and enter a holistic state. We can free ourselves from the more explicit analytical state of "specifics" while thinking and listening to the *total*. We "see" and "hear" the composition in its entirety. When this occurs, appreciation and satisfaction are sensed on an individual and group basis which is directly related to excellence acquired through the analytical mode. This *holistic state* allows us to simultaneously process all this musical information into a total configuration, as opposed to processing separate parts. This state allows us to activate thought toward perception, conceptual images, and expressive qualities.

Perception

Perception is determined by the influences of previous musical experiences. It is becoming aware of qualities through the senses under the influence of all previous musical study, performance, and education. It is the basis for excellence and the means of achieving excellence. Perception determines the end quality.

Conceptual Images

Conceptual images allow us to activate the mental picture of the musical performance we hold in our *minds eye*, which is often abstract rather than realistic. Images create a sense of wholeness and connections of the many details. Images of sound must be a part of our rehearsal structure to fully develop the students musical potential.

Expressive Qualities

The expressive qualities are the slight differences in the way each of us perceive and project our perceptions of a musical composition. These differences express the individuals inner feelings, spirit, character, beauty and meaning. Essentially, the expressive qualities are the result of the interaction between the conductor and performers, relative to the composition and composers intentions.

Too often teaching techniques *fail* to stress the importance of perception, conceptual images, and expressive qualities. *These are difficult concepts to present because students and teachers will frequently lose their patience and revert to the mechanical demands.* We are dealing with things unseen, unheard, or difficult to verbally define. This is the area where all humans are unique in their feelings of emotion. The feelings are internal images and students should not be expected to verbalize these images. *Such an approach will only inhibit the students imaginative abilities and attempt to satisfy the directors description. The images must remain as a personal thought or "picture," and not tampered with by the director.*

Level 5: Summit Experience (Performance)

This is the final step; *an altered state of consciousness through musical expression*. When we function in a holistic state, we become removed somewhat from reality and oblivious to our surroundings. A total involvement of all senses is immersed into the musical expression, with an internal feeling of openness and freedom to make this expression a summit experience. It is an awareness which is perceived as quite different from ordinary consciousness.

When all previous procedures have been developed, the students can "free" themselves from the verbal, analytical, mathematical mode of thinking and allow the images of beauty, emotion, and expressive qualities of the Right Hemisphere to take over. We are totally unaware of time or being, only of *DOING*........ being totally immersed in the musical expression.

This state of consciousness is commonly referred to as the "summit or spiritual" experience. This summit, or peak experience is a basic necessity of all human beings. It is the reason for study, practice, and knowledge. Continued occurrences of this "state" encourages and motivates the student into greater involvement, accomplishment, and expectations. No longer does there exist a "mystery" or "resistance" to new directions, learning, or materials. Patience, practice, and attention to the finest detail takes on greater significance and importance to the student. The performer is motivated to further musical accomplishment and is open to new directions and experiences presented by the teacher.

To achieve this level, or develop teaching techniques to impart such experiences, requires the teacher to have experienced such subtle and sensitive awareness to the art of musical expression. It is the directors *perception* which is the key ! The director's perception was shaped throughout all his early experiences in performance and learning. If these early experiences constantly focused attention to only the mechanical, or mathematical details of the band or orchestra literature, then the directors sensitivity to such expression will tend to be more analytical-mathematical.

Levels 4 and 5 are the points in which the conductor shapes his interpretation of the composers intent. In a sense, he is bringing the student performers into his world of expression and emotional reaction to the literature. This is where the uniqueness and differences of musical expression are found.

If a guest conductor works with your organization, he should not have to address the first three levels if the students have been properly prepared. A guest conductor should only address his inner perception of the composers intent (levels 4 and 5), and allow the students to enter his world of expression and emotional interpretation.

Director Awareness Scale

The following graphic illustration of the five levels described, creates an *Awareness Scale of Time* from *Rehearsal* to *Performance*. The "time" frame (from the beginning of preparation to performance), will vary and cannot be placed into a specific day to day sequence. The graphic illustration creates an awareness as to when and where we deal with the expressive qualities of music. Again, I must stress, each level is not as specific as the graph illustrates. We shift back and forth between levels as we move toward the concert performance or "Peak" experience.

This scale serves one purpose. *It creates a visual image of time, relative to all the rehearsal and instructional procedures, thus determining how this time was used in achieving an effective artistic performance.*

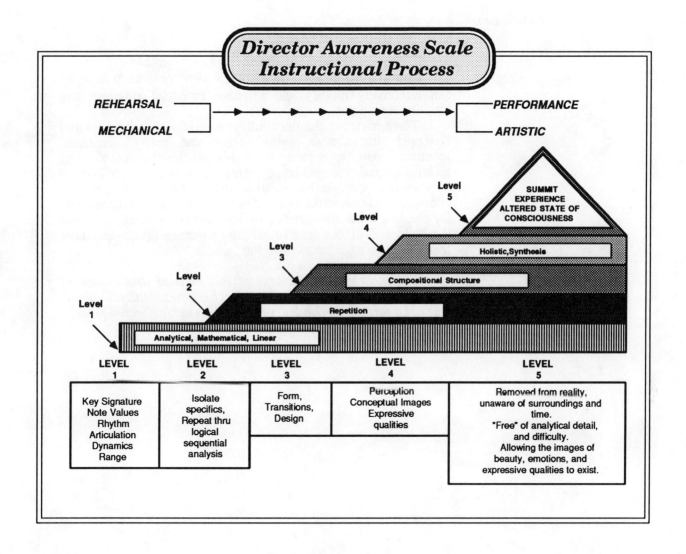

Conclusion

This chapter establishes a greater awareness as to how we can effectively modify and improve rehearsal structure and teaching techniques.

The remaining chapters outline a variety of techniques and concepts that "break away" from the many unrelated, repetitious patterns we may have subconsciously created. The techniques and concepts integrate mental and musical activity to achieve our perceived musical qualities. The entire approach attempts to clarify effective and superior musical performance. By creating a wholistic and spatial awareness we can see where the "bits and pieces" are in relation to other things and how these parts go together to form the "whole."

The most exciting aspect of this method and system of musical learning is that every student becomes totally involved. It is not a forced, demanded, or dictated teaching technique !

Chapter 2

Activating Concentration

Circle of 4ths

Duration Exercises

Grouping Instruments

Chord Qualities

Full Ensemble Scale Performance

Compressing Key Tonality

Digital Patterns

Dominant to Major Key Relationships

The exercises and concepts in this text are designed to focus and control the student's thinking process. When we first initiate this system of musical learning, we must remove all forms of written notation which trigger a physical or mechanical reaction to fingerings, note duration, rhythm, dynamics, articulation, etc. The only reference the students will have on their music stands will be the Circle of 4ths sheet and Grouping assignments (included in Chapter 9). This allows the student to develop auditory skills by re-directing attention primarily to pitch and its characteristics of quality, intonation, balance and blend, instead of the written notation. *The student will be "free" to experience a totally different mental and auditory reaction which creates an increased awareness and sensitivity to musical performance.* Later in this text, the student's listening skills are activated to include not only pitch, but also rhythm patterns, phrasing, dynamics and all the fundamentals of total ensemble sound.

It is important that the letter symbols found on the Circle of 4ths sheet be used in place of musical notation. By having the students react to letter symbols alerts a sensory response which requires visual imagery. This creates a mental image of pitch location on the music staff. *Imaging is an important element in effective learning and memory. Retention and recall are directly effected by the ability to "Image."* The students are perceiving the description through a linear (left) process which activates a visual image in their right hemisphere for greater retention. *It is the "Image" that is retained and recalled for long term memory. The goal is to achieve a mental and auditory reaction while producing a pitch.*

The students first reaction will be quite different from the normal habits established. While some will not have any problems in following this assignment, some will be confused. The students have traditionally been conditioned to reading music from the printed page and tend to become lost and lose confidence when the musical notation is removed. *This approach will develop confidence in what they are "hearing" and focus all attention to the quality of sound they are making !!*

This teaching technique allows the band director to *"Activate, Sustain, and Control"* the students thinking process throughout the rehearsal with maximum musical productivity.

Activating means to engage the students mind toward a particular task, followed by *sustaining* this thought process and not allowing anything to interfere with the task, and lastly, being able to *control* this thought process with time on task to produce the expected results.

Introducing the Circle of 4ths

The entire design of *"ALTERNATIVE REHEARSAL TECHNIQUES"* is based upon the Circle of 4ths. Once students can play through the Circle in unison (or octaves), and reading the written letter symbols (not musical notation) then the director can apply and create unlimited variations to the structure of rehearsal.

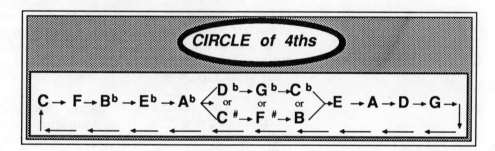

Teaching Procedure:

1.   Distribute the Circle of 4ths Sheet to every band member (Duplicate the number of copies needed from Chapter 9). ONLY refer to the Circle pitches at this time.

2.   Explain to the students that they will NOT be reading musical notation, but responding to the letter symbol, such as C, F, Bb, etc.

3. It is not important at this time whether the students *ascend* or *descend* to the next note in the Circle. The importance should be focused upon reacting and playing a specific pitch. With advanced organizations and players, the director may specify the direction. These players will not have any difficulty with this assignment. *The goal is to simply achieve a mental and auditory reaction while producing a pitch.*

The Circle is written in a traditional reading situation, from left to right.

$$\text{C} \quad \text{F} \quad \text{Bb} \quad \text{Eb} \quad \text{Ab} \quad \overset{\text{Db}}{\underset{\text{C\#}}{\text{or}}} \quad \overset{\text{Gb}}{\underset{\text{F\#}}{\text{or}}} \quad \overset{\text{Cb}}{\underset{\text{B}}{\text{or}}} \quad \text{E} \quad \text{A} \quad \text{D} \quad \text{G} \quad \text{C}$$

I have placed Db, Gb, and Cb above C#, F# and B. *This is only to simplify the students understanding of scales.* Inform students that when they come to these pitches, it is not important whether they think of Flats or Sharps. The C# major scale sounds the same and is fingered the same as the Db major scale. The difference is only in the thought process and musical notation.

4. The director will always use concert pitch when referring to the Circle. If your students are unaware of their instrument transposition, then you will have to specify that instrument's starting pitch on the Circle.

5. Start the Circle on Bb Concert (this being a traditional pitch for Bands creates a bit more comfort and ease for the students), students make their transposition and start at that point. *Clearly define that they will read from left to right and follow the pitches until they return to their starting note. It does not matter where the starting point is on the Circle.*

| Example: |
| C or non-transposing Instruments |

$$\text{Bb} \quad \text{Eb} \quad \text{Ab} \quad \overset{\text{Db}}{\underset{\text{C\#}}{\text{or}}} \quad \overset{\text{Gb}}{\underset{\text{F\#}}{\text{or}}} \quad \overset{\text{Cb}}{\underset{\text{B}}{\text{or}}} \quad \text{E} \quad \text{A} \quad \text{D} \quad \text{G} \quad \text{C} \quad \text{F} \quad \text{(Bb)}$$

Bb Instruments

C F Bb Eb Ab $\begin{array}{c}\textbf{Db}\\ \text{or}\\ \textbf{C\#}\end{array}$ $\begin{array}{c}\textbf{Gb}\\ \text{or}\\ \textbf{F\#}\end{array}$ $\begin{array}{c}\textbf{Cb}\\ \text{or}\\ \textbf{B}\end{array}$ E A D G (C)

Eb Instruments

G C F Bb Eb Ab $\begin{array}{c}\textbf{Db}\\ \text{or}\\ \textbf{C\#}\end{array}$ $\begin{array}{c}\textbf{Gb}\\ \text{or}\\ \textbf{F\#}\end{array}$ $\begin{array}{c}\textbf{Cb}\\ \text{or}\\ \textbf{B}\end{array}$ E A D (G)

F Instruments

F Bb Eb Ab $\begin{array}{c}\textbf{Db}\\ \text{or}\\ \textbf{C\#}\end{array}$ $\begin{array}{c}\textbf{Gb}\\ \text{or}\\ \textbf{F\#}\end{array}$ $\begin{array}{c}\textbf{Cb}\\ \text{or}\\ \textbf{B}\end{array}$ E A D G C (F)

6. When playing the above, inform students to play pitches in a comfortable range. After a short time, you will recognize that the students will adapt to (and learn) the traditional sequence (all ascending or all descending).

7. The entire band will play the above sequence of pitches using whole notes at a tempo not to exceed quarter note = 60. This tempo will allow sufficient time to think of each pitch and look ahead to prepare for the upcoming pitch.

It is extremely important that a day to day pattern not be established with the above exercise. When working with the Circle and unison patterns, change the duration each day. *Remember, we are removing and preventing "NON-THINKING" approaches to the daily warm-up routine.*

The following examples of Duration will assist you with the introduction of this technique. The examples given sustain the pitch for 4, 5, 7, and 9 counts. Inform students that while they are sustaining, they will mentally count 1-2-3-4 (or 5, 7, 9) and the release of each pitch will be *when the "mind" thinks of 4, 5, 7, or 9 (last number).* The purpose is not to relate to any form or note value, but to sustain and think through the total number of beats for each pitch in the Circle of 4ths. *Do not conduct any type of pattern, only a "down beat" to maintain the pulse.*

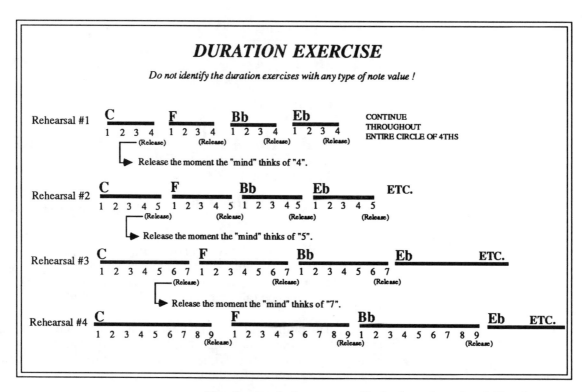

Number variations are unlimited, and as the daily changes are made, the students will be mentally involved in this process. The director should be aware of the behavior changes (attention, concentration, less talking, interest) that will immediately develop. Notably, the students will respond with a renewed interest and increased power of concentration.

As you proceed through this text, you will recognize that all musical elements and concepts are interwoven, connected, and may be approached from any direction which the director chooses (see diagram on page x).

At the end of this text (Chapter 9, page 151) you will find a series of interrelated warm-up procedures outlined for your rehearsals. This will help you in developing a process specifically designed for your organization. You are encouraged to use this segment, and eventually, you will adapt your own patterns as you become familiarized with this entire text.

Grouping Instruments

The instrument grouping assignments allow you to create a variety of approaches to the fundamentals of ensemble performance. The groups are determined by the part the student plays in band. They have been divided into woodwind, brass and percussion choirs so they may be applied in sectionals or group lesson settings. The percussion assignments encourage only keyboard instruments and timpani with the softest mallets available. The reason for such a departure from normal percussion expectations is to emphasize the *internal ensemble pulse* instead of the rhythmic pulse of percussion. This is defined in Chapter 5.

The grouping assignments below appear on the Circle of 4ths Sheet which is distributed to the students. The placement of instruments in the four groups is relevant to the listening concepts presented in Chapter 3 dealing with Aural and Visual Images of Sound. See page 162 for Jazz Ensemble, Orchestra and Chorus Grouping Assignments.

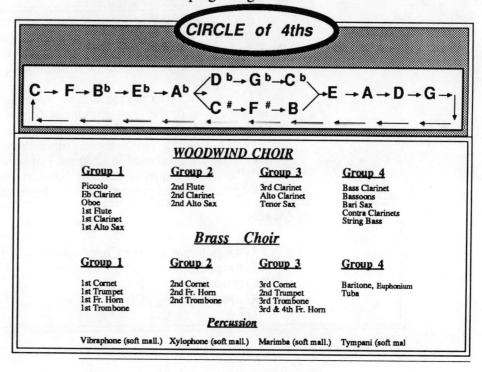

CIRCLE of 4ths

C → F → B♭ → E♭ → A♭ ⟨ D♭ → G♭ → C♭ / C♯ → F♯ → B ⟩ E → A → D → G →

WOODWIND CHOIR

Group 1	Group 2	Group 3	Group 4
Piccolo	2nd Flute	3rd Clarinet	Bass Clarinet
Eb Clarinet	2nd Clarinet	Alto Clarinet	Bassoons
Oboe	2nd Alto Sax	Tenor Sax	Bari Sax
1st Flute			Contra Clarinets
1st Clarinet			String Bass
1st Alto Sax			

Brass Choir

Group 1	Group 2	Group 3	Group 4
1st Cornet	2nd Cornet	3rd Cornet	Baritone, Euphonium
1st Trumpet	2nd Fr. Horn	2nd Trumpet	Tuba
1st Fr. Horn	2nd Trombone	3rd Trombone	
1st Trombone		3rd & 4th Fr. Horn	

Percussion

Vibraphone (soft mall.)	Xylophone (soft mall.)	Marimba (soft mall.)	Tympani (soft mal

Chord Qualities

The students can determine their group assignment by finding, on the Circle of 4ths sheet, the part which they play in band. By assigning a starting pitch for each group, the Circle of 4ths can be played in any type of chord quality. The organization can play all chords in the first attempt. *It is important to note at this time, the grouping assignments for Major Chords is done AFTER the entire ensemble can play the Circle of 4ths in unisons and octaves.*

Example:

Major Chords -	**Group 1**	start Circle on	**Bb**	concert.
	Group 2	"	"	"	**D**	"
	Group 3	"	"	"	**F**	"
	Group 4	"	"	"	**Bb**	"

Each group will proceed through the entire sequence of pitches until they return to their assigned starting pitch (Remember: students must make their instrument transpositions, or you will have to designate each transposing instrument pitch).

This teaching technique allows your band to perform *all major chords* with the least amount of complications. *You are free to address balance, blend, tone quality, etc.* Specific approaches dealing with these fundamentals of ensemble performance are presented in Chapter 3 of this text.

When your students become comfortable with the Major Chord Qualities, then proceed with the following:

Minor Chord Quality

Group 1	start on	**Bb**	Concert, continue through Circle.
Group 2	" "	**Db**	"	"	"	"
Group 3	" "	**F**	"	"	"	"
Group 4	" "	**Bb**	"	"	"	"

Dominant 7th Chords

        Group 1 start Circle on **Ab** Concert
        Group 2   "   "   "   **D**
        Group 3   "   "   "   **F**
        Group 4   "   "   "   **Bb**

Major 7th Chords

        Group 1 start Circle on **A** Concert
        Group 2   "   "   "   **D**
        Group 3   "   "   "   **F**
        Group 4   "   "   "   **Bb**

Minor 7th Chords

        Group 1 start Circle on **Ab** Concert
        Group 2   "   "   "   **Db**
        Group 3   "   "   "   **F**
        Group 4   "   "   "   **Bb**

Diminished 7th Chords

        Group 1 start Circle on **G** Concert
        Group 2   "   "   "   **E**
        Group 3   "   "   "   **Db**
        Group 4   "   "   "   **Bb**

*see Chapter 9 for additional Chord Grouping Variations

The director must vary the approaches with the above chord qualities for each rehearsal. Most important, *do not hurry through all chord quality examples.* It is important that the students are allowed sufficient time to develop their listening skills (Refer and apply concepts of Chapter 3, Creating an Aural and Visual Image of Sound).

Daily rehearsal variations with chord qualities are done through duration, dynamics and rhythm patterns. (Refer to Chapter 4, Measurement of Sound and Silence and Odd Numbers for additional variations). As you proceed through this text, the variations will expand to include any and all literature demands.

The next two pages include some very basic rhythm patterns which should be implemented after your students have been familiarized with playing through the Circle of 4ths in unison and major chord qualities. More examples are given in Chapter 9.

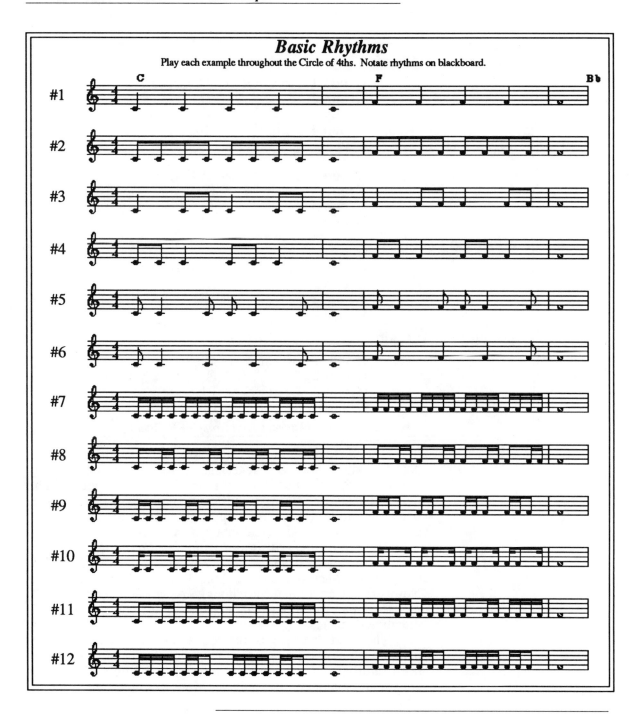

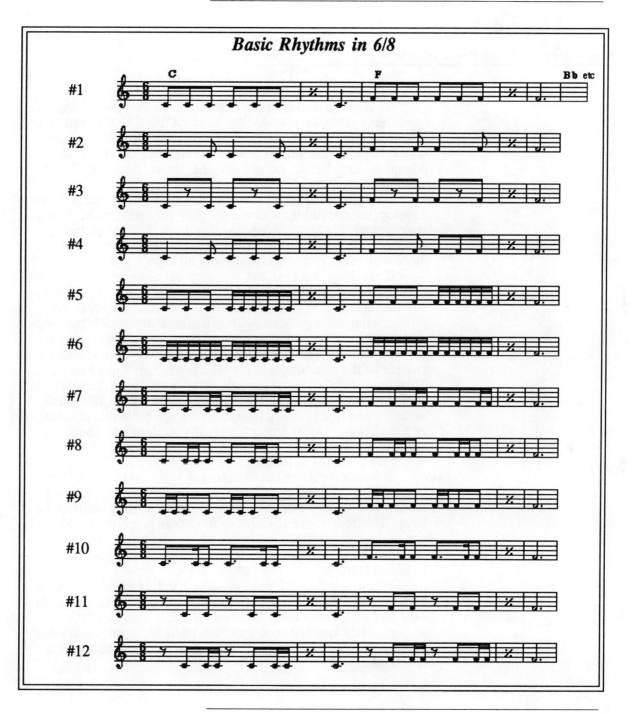

Basic Rhythms in 6/8

Full Ensemble Scale Performance

A concern most often expressed is the limitations of bands only able to play in the keys of F, Bb, Eb, and Ab. Warm-up procedures most often are only directed to these major keys. This places severe limitations on the students potential and limits access to the most prominent band literature.

The goal of this segment in the warm-up process is to develop an ensemble which can play all major and minor scales, and not just those in flat keys. The techniques described are designed for bands with limited ability as well as those with mastery and proficiency in all keys.

If we look back at the students early experiences with major scales it is understandable why some reach high school without being able to perform all major scales. These early instructional settings start with a major scale which has one sharp or flat. The student is to learn or memorize this scale for the next lesson. The following lesson typically introduces the student to the next major scale which has two sharps or flats. This procedure continues week after week with hopes that someday all scales will be played. This "system" usually breaks down due to many factors which are quite discouraging to the student. Most importantly, the student has shaped an attitude and belief that the Db, Gb, Cb, C#, F#, and B major scales are the most difficult.

Students receive limited exposure to the so called difficult keys. This limited experience usually deals with only the etudes and studies found in lesson books dealing with those keys. I believe those students who experience such problems are the result of "teacher imposed restrictions" and *not* the students lack of ability to comprehend scale structure or technical facility.

When using the Circle of 4ths for full ensemble scale performance, *those students unable to play all scales should play and sustain the roots or keynotes while the others play the scales*. They quickly recognize the need for such knowledge when you continue through the scale variations generated each rehearsal day.

For those students who are having difficulty with scales, the instructional procedure outlined below will assure the student and teacher of complete scale understanding. It is based upon a very simple learning process and should be applied first in a small group lesson setting.

Teaching Procedure:

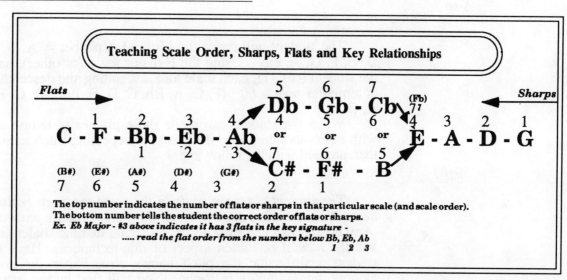

*Please note and alert the students that the order of flats is opposite the order of sharps. The sharp order and number starts below F# and proceeds to the left.

This system of scale development will always assure correct order of flats and sharps in a key signature.

FLAT KEYS:
The numbers above each pitch correspond with the numbers below. F major scale has 1 flat (#1 above the pitch F) and the name of that flat is Bb (#1 below the pitch Bb). Cb major has 7 flats (#7 above the pitch Cb), the 7th flat is Fb (#7 below Fb in parenthesis), the order of flats are Bb, Eb, Ab, Db, Gb, Cb, Fb. The Cb major scale sounds the same as B major which has 5 sharps.

SHARP KEYS:

G major scale has 1 sharp (#1 above the pitch G) and the name of that sharp is F# (#1 below the pitch F#). C# major scale has 7 sharps (#7 above C#), the 7th sharp is B (#7 below the pitch B), the order of sharps are F#, C#, G#, D#, A#, E#, B#. The C# major scale sounds the same as the Db major scale which has 5 flats.

Step 2

The student will recite the Musical Alphabet = A, B, C, D, E, F, G, A, etc. Using the F major scale (or other), have the student RECITE each scale tone, ascending and descending at a quarter note = 60 (F, G, A, Bb, C, D, E, F, E, D, C, Bb, A, G, F).

When the student can recite these pitches in tempo and with ease (no stumbling, stuttering, or repeating pitch names) then proceed with the following:

Step 3

The student plays the scale in the same tempo as recited, and mentally recites each pitch as the scale is being played !! Any breakdown that may occur is a signal that the student has lost the *mental recitation* aspect of this technique. Have the student again recite the pitch names also, *finger the notes without any hesitation in tempo.* You will find by the second or third try, the student will have total command of this mental process and will perform each scale with complete accuracy. Always start over if the student hesitates or stutters when reciting the pitches in tempo. *The importance is to establish a "timed" mental flow of pitch recitation.*

Step 4

The next important step is to have the student play the scale again, in the same pulse and mental recitation, but this time focus attention on the *"PHYSICAL FEEL"* (finger movement). *STRESS the "FEELING"* as they play the scale. *This is most important in developing sensory connections to improve memory !! Remember how the scale "FEELS IN YOUR FINGERS" !*

30

Step 5

Continue this process with *all major scales*. The student is capable of playing all major scales, without error, in one lesson setting. At no time (in full band rehearsal or lessons) should you address any scale as being difficult ! Don't "impose" scale difficulty on the students.

The students should be aware of reacting to scales in two forms; letter names (A, B, C, D,etc.) and scale steps numerically (1, 2, 3, 4, 5, etc.). *The numerical identity is used when expanding this system to Digital Patterns.*

Scale Variation Exercises

Review the exercises and note the asterisk at specific points in each scale. This is the point at which the director must inform students to specifically think and prepare for the *next key ! They no longer focus attention on the scale they are playing (that's completed), only sustaining the last pitch while thinking of the upcoming scale. The direction, "fix the next key in your mind," is given while the band is sustaining the last note of each scale.* After several scales, the students will automatically start thinking of the *next* scale and you no longer have to remind them of where they are to think of the next key.

The scale examples are not written in every major key, only the rhythmic variations you will use in the development of this technique. *Always have the full band play through every major scale with the specified variation. Change the rhythm for each rehearsal.* The variations are written from simple to complex. *Do not write the scales out for the students....* if this happens, you will have destroyed the entire process of effective learning.

Scale Variations

Play each example throughout the Circle of 4ths

* The asterisk is the point at which you must inform the students to specifically think and prepare for the NEXT KEY !

Scale Variations (cont.)

Alternate Ascending and Descending Scales

The next level of scale performance will have the students *ascending* the first scale and *descending* the next. By alternating scales in this manner (without written notation), the students response and reactions are fully engaged and directed to listening, technical facility, and ease of performance. *This process continues throughout the Circle of 4ths.*

Review the exercises carefully. The scales are written in pairs. The first of every two examples are *Ascending* the first, and *Descending* the next while the scales just below start with *Descending* first, and *Ascending* the next.

Alternating Ascending and Descending

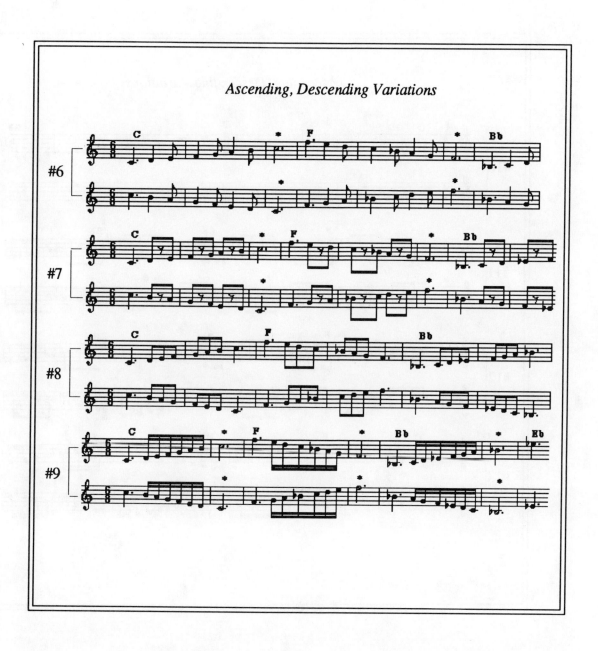

Ascending, Descending Variations

Ascending, Descending Variations

Compressing Key Tonality with Digital Patterns

When your band becomes proficient with full ensemble scale performance, the next logical step in mental and technical development is through digital patterns. Digital patterns are used extensively in improvisation and the training of a jazz musician. *This rehearsal technique allows the musician to gain technical facility with a spontaneous reaction to all scales, keys, and chord qualities.* By using a similar approach with the entire band playing unison digital patterns, a musical awareness and understanding is developed which allows your program to grow significantly.

Compressing Key Tonality is directly related to *Digital Patterns*. The term simply means: reducing the amount of time (beats or measures) played in any given key. *The goal is to create a spontaneous mental reaction and response to all keys through digital patterns.*

Throughout the students normal training, a mental process was established which only allowed the student to think of one key for 4, 8, 12, 16 or more measures. Many etudes, technical exercises, and scales are played for "x" number of measures or beats. The students mind only functioned in that particular key for the number of beats or measures. This is an unrealistic situation when performing wind literature which may have technical passages that call for the musician to have the facility to respond to all keys.

The ability to spontaneously react and recognize various scale fragments and passages reduces the amount of time the student will be involved in repetitious, technical practice. It also provides greater accuracy in sight reading.

The structure of this segment in rehearsal techniques will develop such immediate reaction, technical facility and improved sight reading for the student musician. *The technique starts the students mentally processing "numbers" relative to "pitch" slowly. As the tempo increases, the processing naturally shifts to an auditory function.* The students concentration is constantly engaged throughout this process. An auditory perception is developed and is significantly different from the standard reading approach. The patterns are not written in standard musical notation. Without the written musical notation, the student cannot do anything but *think* and *listen*. They must rely on their mental capabilities.

As the students skill and understanding develops, you should point out various technical passages within the literature the band is preparing. This connection is important in the early stages. Later, when a technical problem exists, all you need to do is prompt the student to analyze the passage through digital patterns and keys. *The student can scan new music and relate to keys and sequences instead of individual notes.* A considerable amount of time is saved with repetitious practice when students can respond analytically to technical passages and find digital sequences.

Be patient and establish a slow tempo in the beginning stages so as the students will have time to mentally process and react. You will immediately become aware of an intense form of concentration developing. Mistakes will be made in the keys of Db, Gb, etc., but this is only a temporary situation. This entire approach will remove the insecurity and inhibitions to those keys.

The sequences start at a very basic level of thought process and expands to more complex figures. It is not unrealistic to have your entire band performing complex digital patterns within a short period of time. You are encouraged to create your own digital patterns as the students progress.

Teaching Procedure:

Do not write the Digital Patterns in standard musical notation. *Only give the students the number sequence and rhythms which they will process for each key while playing through the Circle of 4ths.* The importance and significance of this rehearsal procedure emphasizes the students concentration, pitch awareness, melodic comprehension and retention abilities. *Without the traditional written notation, an entirely new listening awareness is being developed.* Starting at a very slow mechanical process, and as tempo increases, we gradually shift to an auditory process.

Exercise #1   **1-2-1-2-1** (written on blackboard or defined to students).

Description: Students will process 1st and 2nd degrees of each major scale. While sustaining the whole note (last note of each pattern), they will be mentally preparing for the next key. As stated on page 32, we are "compressing the time" in which the performer has to process a particular key.

Exercise #2   1-2-3-2-1

Description: Students process 1st, 2nd, and 3rd degrees of each scale. Remind students while sustaining the last whole note of each scale they will prepare for the next key.

Exercise #3   1-2-3-2-1-3-1
Description: Similar to Ex. #2. This exercise extends the mental control and directs attention to the 3rd degree of each scale. The 3rd degree of each scale in this exercise is the note they will "turn around" to return to the 1st scale step. When they return, they must remember that pitch and play in half notes (1-3) before returning to the Tonic or Keynote. This exercise is the initial preparation for effective triad and chord performance in all major keys for the entire organization. It is also a means in which scale steps and interval awareness b ecomes a part of the musical process. Without going into standard theoretical detail, the student forms pitch relationships relative to key tonality.

Exercise #4   1-2-1-2-1-2-3-2-1
Description: This is a combination of exercises #1 and #2. Its purpose is to extend the concentration, pitch awareness, melodic comprehension and retention abilities of the students.

Exercise #5   1-2-3-4-5-4-3-2-1
Description: Awareness is now directed to the 5th degree of each scale. This digital pattern is important once students develop a moderate amount of skill in processing this pattern. It is most significant in the development of full ensemble technical facility and articulation clarity. Various articulation patterns are easily adapted to this digital pattern.

Exercise #6   1-2-3-4-5-4-3-2-1-3-5-3-1
Description: This exercise is an extension of #3. The ensemble is introduced to the performance of Triads in each Key. I have found the following description to be sufficient for student understanding: " As you ascend the scale, remember the 3rd degree and the top note (5th) which you turnaround on. Then play 1-3-5-3 in half notes followed by the Tonic (whole note).

Exercise #7   1-2-3-4-5-4-3-2-1-3-5-8-5-3-1
Description: A further extension of #6 and the development of full ensemble chord performance (and understanding through a logical sequence !)

Exercise #8   1-3-5-8-5-3-1
Description: An extension of exercise #7. Knowledge and performance of the pitches in the major chord quality.

Exercise #9   1-3-5-6-5-4-3-2-1
Description: This pattern reinforces triad performance while extending and becoming aware of the 6th scale degree.

41

Exercise #10   1-6-5-4-3-2-1
Description: An extension of exercise #9 and performing the interval of the major 6th.

Exercise #11   1-7-1-7-1
Description: Introducing and becoming aware of the 7th scale degree.

Exercise #12   1-8-7-8-1
Description: Reinforcing the octave and introducing the pitch relationship of the 7th degree.

Exercise #13   1-3-5-7-8-7-5-3-1
Description: Introducing the sound and creating an auditory awareness of the major 7th chord quality.

The example descriptions give you an understanding of the Digital Pattern learning sequence for full ensemble performance. As you review the exercises, you will readily see the expansion to other intervals and the effectiveness of this warm-up instructional technique. This is a very simple, logical learning progression which creates greater meaning and worth to the student in their performance abilities.

CAUTION !

The Digital Patterns are played at a slow quarter note tempo (quarter = 60). This gives the student time to mentally react and process each of the pitches. As student reaction time improves, gradually increase tempo and change patterns to eighth and sixteenth notes. *As tempo increases, this is where the "shift" occurs from a mechanical to an auditory process !*

Be consistent in reminding the students to think of the next key while playing the last note of each digital pattern (keynote). This is critical in you instructional techniques. Too often we neglect to define the thought process involved and assume the students will effectively respond.

Do not duplicate the musical notation written for these examples. This is strictly a mental and auditory process....not a mechanical or visual reaction to signs and symbols !

Digital Patterns are not to be introduced until the ensemble has moderate performance ability with all major scales.

It is important to note that it will take your organization a few months of rehearsals to gain mental and technical facility of all 13 Digital Pattern Exercises. I can assure you that all students are capable of this process and the rewards are tremendous.

When your students become comfortable with the quarter note digital patterns, move to the 8th and 16th note patterns found on the following pages.

Eighth Note Digital Patterns

Eighth Note Digitals (cont.)

Sixteenth Note Digital Patterns

Sixteenth Note Digitals (cont.)

Dominant to Major Key Relationships

Digital Pattern Exercises #11, #12, and #13 are the logical steps in teaching Dominant to Tonic relaionships. W e simply use the Circle of 4ths and alternate the thinking process between each key.

Teaching Procedure:

1. Review and play exercise #11 throughout the Circle of 4ths. After performing #11 in major keys, define to the students that this time they will "think" of flatting or lowering scale step 7 by a half step. Allow them some time to process this first before playing. Further define that the b7th is the 4th degree of the next key.
2. Exercise #11 now becomes: 1-b7-1-b7- 1.

3. Exercise #12 becomes 1-8-b7-8-1

4. Play exercises #11 and #12 several times before proceeding to adjust exercise #13.

5. Exercise #13 is now played as 1-3-5-b7-8-b7-5-3-1.

Once the students become comfortable in processing the lowered 7th in each key, they have developed the necessary foundation for performing Dominant 7ths to Major. This procedure is simply alternating between Exercise #8 and Altered Exercise #13. The success with this series of exercises is determined by allowing the students time to mentally process each interval and digital pattern.

1. Return and review Exercise #8.

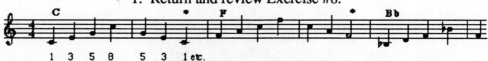

2. Define to students that they will now play Exercise #13 in the first key (Bb) followed by playing Exercise # 8 in the next key.

Digital Pattern will be:
(C) 1-3-5-b7-8-b7-5-3-1, (F) 1-3-5-8-5-3-1, (Bb) 1-3-5-b7-8-b7-5-3-1, (Eb) etc.

Alternate this sequence so as all Dominant 7th and Majors are performed.

Digital Pattern will be:
(C) 1-3-5-8-5-3-1, (F) 1-3-5-b7-8-b7-5-3-1, (Bb) 1-3-5-8-5-3-1, etc.

Conclusion

Carefully review this chapter. Your understanding will be critical to the success of the instructional techniques presented in the following chapters. You should be forewarned and not attempt to undergo all the exercises in a hurried fashion. *Each one is carefully built on the preceding and is a logical sequential thinking process.* Any type of short cut or abbreviated presentation will confuse the issue.

The entire process is unlike any other method book. This system of musical learning is a result of careful study, practice and many years of working with my own students and serving as a guest conductor with all levels of student musicians. I guarantee you positive results with these concepts and techniques. Combining your patience with this system of musical learning will produce a complete or total musician with all the superior qualities of musical expression.

Chapter 3

Creating an Aural
and
Visual Image of Sound

Visualization, Imagery

Horizontal Sound Structure

Vertical Sound Structure

Chord Color

Your introductory experiences with the exercises in Chapter 2 have established a foundation for Alternative Rehearsal Techniques. This chapter deals with concepts and techniques which clarify the structure of ensemble sound through many new approaches. They are to be implemented into the foundation established in Chapter 2. As you proceed through the remaining pages of this text, the truly *"CREATIVE DIRECTOR"* (you) will emerge !

Aural and Visual Image of Sound

Scientific research points out the fact that the more sensory connections and associations we can make in learning, the greater our retention and recall. The techniques and skills developed in this chapter reinforce learning either through a visual (see) reaction, which alerts an auditory (hear) and physical (feel) response, or an auditory response which creates a visual image and physical reaction. We create a positive learning environment within each rehearsal by subconsciously connecting visual, auditory, and physical (hands, embouchure, breath support, etc.) senses.

Creating an aural and visual image of sound has many significant implications in the development of a superior band program. *The concepts presented on the following pages stress "total" and listening "to and for the whole ensemble sound." Thus, removing the independent or individualized reaction to one specific sound without relationship to the total ensemble texture.* The concepts not only address these concerns, but also create a unification and sensitization of listening skills within the entire band. The organization becomes *unified into one instrument,* with the conductor free to express and shape this unified sound into an artistic expression.

Visualization, Imagery

If there was ever a secret to superior band performance, I believe *visualization* and *imagery* to be the answer and solution to many directors performance concerns. The visualization process cannot be stressed or emphasized enough. *It is the process which connects all details and parts into the "whole."*

When working with these concepts for a short time, the students become comfortable and do not fear mistakes. There is a quietness and intensity in rehearsal situations. The students are attentive and absorbed with your directions. This is the signal of your control over the students concentration. Their minds are open and ready for your input and *programming*. Be extremely cautious of *musical programming,* as it has far reaching and lasting affects and effects ! You will definitely hear it in your next concert performance.

A very significant teaching technique which is encouraged throughout "Alternative Rehearsal Techniques" instructional system is to have the students *close their eyes* while performing the exercises. We often observe professional soloists and jazz musicians playing with their eyes closed. The reason for this is obvious; they remove all visual distractions and are able to perceive, see, and become totally immersed into the expression of music as a "whole."

Stronger learning occurs when the students close their eyes and create their own personal images of sound. They can *"SEE"* Pitch, Balance, Blend, Intonation, Tone Quality, and Total Ensemble Sound in their *MIND'S EYE.* There are no exact images or "pictures" used. It is the uniqueness of this "picture" or image the student creates which is essential, and not what someone else sees, defines, or imposes.

Trying to have students verbally describe what they see in their "minds eye" will destroy the effectiveness of this teaching technique and creative process. The students should not be expected to verbalize these images (don't tamper with this). Allow them to hold their own impressions of sound and its beauty. This is the one most significant factor in the failure of traditional teaching techniques..... the "question-answer" teaching technique inhibits the students response as they try to satisfy the teacher "answer" or description. This process develops a fear of failure.

By having the students close their eyes and perform the many exercises in this text, we remove all distractions of the room, people, and things. *The removal of visual distractions forces the student to focus total attention and concentration to the image of the specific task ..LISTENING !! ..No daydreaming or wandering minds !* Such concepts and techniques prompt the " mode shift " from the super analytical left mode to the beauty and imagery of the right mode. *Through this method, we create a mental picture of sound and a foundation for what we expect in total performance.* Within a short time, you will easily sense the intensity of concentration with the organization. The early stages of these techniques will often lead to some giggling from the students. Don't allow this to discourage or eliminate these teaching concepts.

The next section deals with total ensemble sound through three basic visual concepts. These concepts allow students to more effectively direct their attention and listening to tone quality, intonation, balance, and blend. The three terms are Horizontal Sound Structure, Vertical Sound Structure, and Chord Color.

Horizontal Sound Stucture

Horizontal Sound Structure implies the duration of sound on a horizontal plane, from left to right, similar as in reading. *It starts at the point of Entrance and continues to the Release or "beginning of silence."*
This concept creates an entirely new auditory understanding and "feeling" for sound. *An image of sound is created on a horizontal basis. Its consistency is determined by the auditory skill and the visual exactness of the mental image, which must be supported by the physical senses to create this sound.*

If the mental image of sound is changed by either dynamics, volume, or tempo, the other senses (auditory and physical) must be associated to effectively create the intended performance (mental image).

When applying this concept to rehearsal situations, emphasis is focused on all ingredients of sound; tone quality, balance, blend, intonation, volume and dynamics. Its purpose is to develop a reaction to maintaining this sound from left to right (entrance to release) for the duration of the written sound.

Example:

While playing through major chord qualities around the Circle of 4ths, have students in group 1 (or 2,3,4) release before any of the other groups. It will be immediately apparent what happens when individuals or groups do not sustain through the expected duration of sound. This was the purpose of the duration exercises presented in Chapter 2. *The duration, and specifically releasing a note on a given "number," is critical to achieving uniformity of sound from beginning to end. Consistency of sound and quality can never be achieved if the correct mental process is not established !*

To further emphasize Horizontal Sound, have an individual or group vary the volume from loud to soft while the remainder of the organizations is maintaining one volume. As this is happening, and if you and your students are visualizing the variation and duration of this sound, it will be apparent as to the importance of such a concept in effective listening skills.

Such performance discrepencies are always evident in many organizations. This is because they have only been instructed to hold through the given duration without attention focused to the total ensemble sound. Importance was not focused to the quality of sound throughout the duration. They are not conditioned to the color, quality, density, balance or resulting sound when they do not sustain as a total unit.

Vertical Sound Structure

Vertical Sound Structure is perhaps the most essential listening concept in the development of a superior organization. This term implies sound built on a perpendicular plane. *Its importance and emphasis removes independent interpretation of sound while directing it to the total ensemble sound.* This is most significant in the unification of the organization's auditory skills.

Vertical Sound Structure creates an aural response to the "total" or "whole" ensemble sound from bottom to top (tuba to piccolo) relative to entrance, release, and rhythmic subdivision. All ingredients of sound; tone quality, balance, blend, intonation, volume and dynamics, are maintained relative to the quality and texture of sound from bottom to top.

The visual image that is created of the band sound from tuba to piccolo triggers the auditory response which must be supported by the physical response to maintain the consistency and quality of this visual image. This too can be altered by dynamics, volume, tempo and, the compositional voicing or scoring.

Example:

While playing through major chord qualities around the Circle of 4ths, have students in group 4 play at a "PP" level while students in group 1 play at a "FF" level. This will immediately make the students aware of what the term Vertical Sound structure means and how constant attention and listening must be focused to the *fundamental* or support groups in creating a total ensemble sound. Through this approach, proper balance and blend is taught.

After the "incorrect" approach has been played, return and play correctly with group 4 playing at a "F" level while group 1 plays at a "MP" or "MF" level. It will be apparent immediately of what the responsibilities are of the students when listening and playing with the concept of *vertical sound structure*.

Rhythmic subdivision is another important element which is more effectively taught through Vertical Sound Structure. Rhythmic clarity and definition must also be maintained on a perpendicular plane from Tuba to Piccolo. Exercises and instructional techniques are presented in Chapter 5.

The two concepts, Horizontal and Vertical Sound Structure, unify the students listening skills and they no longer function as "individuals" but as "one complete instrument." This concept eliminates the top-heavy, strident, individual sounds, over-powering, and the "out of tune" band sound.

Another significant teaching perception of Horizontal and Vertical Sound Structure is discussed in Chapter 5 which deals with the application of these concepts through the "Ruler of Time." It is extremely important that your instructional techniques be related with these concepts.

Chord Color

The term *CHORD COLOR* implies texture and quality relative to tone quality, balance, blend, intonation, and volume. Chord Color is based upon the individual, the section, and the total ensemble sound.

Chord Color is determined by the strength and quality of the FUNDAMENTAL while placing the 5th of the chord "within" the Fundamental (which becomes a part of the fundamental or an overtone of the fundamental) and lastly, placing the COLOR TONES of the 3rd, 7th, etc. The color tones determine the quality of the chord (major, minor, diminished, etc.). *The volume of Color Tones plays a significant role in Balance and Blend.*

TEXTURE is determined by the composer's voicings. For instance, the texture of sound projected in Holst, Mennin, Copland, Dahl, Husa, McBeth, Bennett are each uniquely different. Each composer's unique characteristic of total ensemble sound has been created through the variation of voicings (transparency to density) by the doubling and placement of overtones and color tones.

Example:

While playing through major chord qualities around the Circle of 4ths, have students in groups 1, 3 and 4 play play at a "PP" level while group 2 plays at a "FF" level. The results will dramatically show how proper balance is achieved. A more profound example can be demonstrated by playing Dominant Seventh Chords with Group 1 playing at a FF level while the other groups play at MP.

Correct the above by having only groups 1, 3 and 4 play and then bring in group 2 with a hand signal and increase or decrease the volume of sound until it is balanced to your liking.

Experiment with different dynamic levels with groups and individuals. Listen to the "color" changes when individuals or sections are not playing "inside" the total ensemble sound. The term "Chord Color" has more significance to students than other terms to identify quality of total ensemble sound.

Conclusion

The terms Horizontal Sound Structure, Vertical Sound Structure, and Chord Color activate a mental and auditory process to 3 significant factors in the development of superior ensemble performance. These 3 area's are:

a. *Creating an Aural (hear) and Visual (see) Image of sound from eft to right, or in the direction of the sound.*

b. *Creating an Aural (hear) and Visual (see) Image of sound from bottm to top (tuba to piccolo).*

c. *Creating an Aural (hear) and Visual (see) Image of Color and Texture of this sound in a wholistic concept.*

58

The three listening concepts, (horizontal, vertical, chord color) are best presented through *incorrect* methods followed by the director shaping and tailoring the sound to the desired expectations. As the total ensemble sound is shaped, the director must impress upon the students to *visualize the sound*.

These terms are totally integrated relative to the structure of band sound. *Their use creates a positive learning experience and recall is immediate.*

The terms are used with the Circle of 4ths and chord qualities. Your rehearsal techniques will be more productive if all your demands and expectations of proper balance and blend are established at the beginning of rehearsal through these three concepts. Their use activates an awareness to total ensemble sound instead of specific sections or individuals.

The following chapters expand on these concepts and integrate teaching procedures to total ensemble sound.

Chapter 4

Ensemble Tone Quality

Superior total ensemble sound and quality is determined by the students auditory skills established through teaching techniques relative to the *fundamental pitch.* By establishing tuning procedures to the *fundamental,* the ensemble's listening skills improve significantly through the concept of *vertical sound* structure (sound from "bottom to top"-tuba to piccolo).

The *fundamental* will always be the lowest voice, part, or section of an organization. *When listening is taking place, the "ear" searches and attempts to balance all upper voices relative to the lowest pitch.* Consequently,. if listening skills are not established relative to the theories of sound or overtone series, conflict will always be present both for the performer and the listener. *All upper pitches must be related to the fundamental....... it is the "basic law of ensemble pitch." Effective Balance, Blend or Intonation cannot be achieved without this understanding.*

Balance and Blend

Balance and blend techniques stabilize the diversity of sounds within the entire ensemble. Effective balance and blend in an ensemble is and must be determined by the *fundamental* or *bass voice.* It is the directors ability to unify individual and section sound volume, tone quality, and intonation relative to this fundamental. *The fundamental is "the basic law of sound."*

Following the *fundamental* regarding importance, the 5th is balanced relative to this *fundamental.* When proper balance is achieved with the *fundamental* and *5th,* the director then "places" the color tones of the 3rd, 7th, 9th. etc. This "tailoring" of sound is done through the Groupings and playing the Circle of 4ths with the various chord qualities. The "tailoring" of your ensemble's overall quality of sound is determined by the director's inner perception of total band sound.

Too often, little attention is given to the bass section of the band. Frequently the tuba section is almost non-existant, extremely sharp in pitch or generally lacks tonal development.   The critical sections of bassoons, contra clarinets, bass clarinets, and baritone saxophone are all part of this *fundamental* and must be treated with the same importance as the tuba section. Not until these sections are strengthened can effective balance and blend be addressed.

Taking this concept to the next degree, consider each section of the band with a Fundamental section (all 3rd or 4th parts) and focus attention to those individuals. With the lower voices of the section playing at a mezzo forte or forte level, the second part is now placed upon this foundation with less volume than the lower voice. Now have the first section play their pitch and not *"pass the sound"* (overpower) of 2nd or 3rd parts.   The improvement of sound will be evident immediately....*the "Laws of Sound" are determined by the fundamental !*

The musical quality of your organization will be determined by the quality of the bass voices and all 3rd and 4th parts. Traditional procedures tend to place the stronger players in the solo and 1st parts. Competing for chair placement reinforces the students attitude to reflect, *the best are in the top chairs*. With this type of philosophy, those students seated in 2nd, 3rd, and 4th parts sub-consciously feel their parts are not as important and the result is poor balance. This type of situation will always exist and is something that cannot be removed. It can be resolved by the director increasing attention and emphasis to these individuals relative to the band's total sound.

Blend is achieved by having two or more sounds mixed so that they cannot be distinguished or separated. It is the ability to have the entire clarinet section, or any other section, to sound as "one" instrument. Blend is determined by the effectiveness of director teaching techniques in establishing student listening skills which lead to a *homogeneous section sound*.

Effective blend is the result of a student being taught properly to listen to his/her sound while being aware of how it becomes a part of the section and total ensemble sound. The *knowing* comes from understanding and making the subtle changes in tone quality so it can become a "part of the whole."

The quality of instrument, mouthpiece, reeds, etc. are significant factors in determining the final "blending" which will be achieved (it is impossible to have a resonite clarinet blend with a grenadilla wood clarinet).

Section balance and blend is developed by using the groupings found on the Circle of 4ths sheet. It can be presented in sectional rehearsals or in a full band rehearsal.

Intonation

Intonation is the one essential fundamental of ensemble quality. It is an auditory skill which causes every band director problems. Students frequently have difficulty in discerning the *sharpness* or *flatness* of a pitch. The actual task is, being able to discern the smallest fluctuations of pitch frequencies (conflicting "beats" of two or more pitches - 440 vps vs. 445 vps) and eliminating such fluctuations. Some students can adjust quickly while others never achieve satisfaction.

The teaching techniques used from the students earliest musical experiences frequently create confusion and problems. *When students are instructed to listen for sharpness or flatness in pitch, the attention is focused to discerning the highness or lowness, instead of the actual beats or misaligned frequencies of two or more sounds !*

Teaching techniques dealing with intonation vary from program to program. Many directors use the visual approach with a strobe tuner (which is an effective approach) for the individual player. Without a follow-up to this technique and the ability to determine relationships within the total ensemble sound, the student becomes sensitized only to their sound and believes to be *in tune*. Pitch discrepancies are more evident with this approach especially in exposed or solo sections. Quite often the pitch will not be within the pitch center established by the *fundamental*. Students are usually able to react to this "out of tuneness," but feel that they are *correct* because they could *stop the strobe* (the others are wrong). *Furthermore, students hesitate to adjust because the strongest tendency is to have greater belief in the "picture of the strobe," instead of the "ear of listening." People do not doubt or question a picture, a picture assures clarity and security while there is considerable reservation and a lack of confidence in what we "hear" regarding pitch.*

With the above description of the structure of intonation, proceed to the actual teaching process used for effective individual and group awareness to intonation. From this point on, the director will refer to intonation as "beatless" tuning.

Developing these techniques will call for small group instructional settings first, followed by similar expectations in the full rehearsal situation.

Teaching Procedure:

Step #1

Choose two students for this demonstration. Describe to the students how two similar pitches create "beats" when they are not vibrating at the same frequency. The director should take one of the instruments and purposely pull the slide or barrel out to create flatness. Student A will sustain an F concert. While the F concert is being sustained, direct student B to enter and sustain the F concert with Student A. Inform the students to listen for the "beats" as they both sustain the F concert. This is usually quite apparent at the outset and students react easily to this situation.

Step #2

Inform the students *not to listen for the sharpness or flatness as* they might have been taught. Listen for the *SPEED OF THE BEATS. The faster the beats = the more OUT of tune......and the slower the beats = the more IN tune.* The goal is to eliminate beats. Beats are eliminated in 2 ways: adjusting the slide or barrel in our out and the second is by embouchure pressure or bending the pitch (firming up or relaxing). Unnecessary pressure on the mouth-piece restricts tone quality. Although students who have instruments with design deficiencies will find it necessary to use pressure for the small adjustments in "beatless tuning."

Step #3

Inform student B to tune to student A by adjusting the barrel or slide until all beats are eliminated, emphasizing again that the faster the beats, the more *out of tune* and the slower the beats, the more *in tune*. Follow the procedures below:

Logical Conclusions to Effective Intonation

1. At this time it is unimportant to recognize sharp or flat, *only the speed of the beats.*

2. Make a move with the barrel, slide, mouthpiece (sax, flute-roll in or out). It doesn't make any difference whether it is in or out. *Listen for the beats, did they slow down or speed up with the barrel or slide adjustment ?*

3. If the beats were faster, *then you made the wrong move, adjust in the opposite direction.*

4. If the beats became slower, *then you are making the correct move, continue until all beats are eliminated.*

5. If you find yourself *"pinching"* to eliminate beats, then *your instrument is too long, it must be shortened.*

6. If you find yourself *"relaxing"* your embouchure to eliminate beats, then *the instrument is too short, it must be lengthened.*

7. When two or more similar pitches are played, the sound is "beatless" (and you are not using any unnecessary pressure or relaxation on the mouthpiece) ....

YOU ARE PERFECTLY IN TUNE !

The sequence of events and results are determined by the individual students *logical conclusions*. The director has defined and described the sequence of events and the student arrives at the correct conclusion. Effective learning has taken place. Visualization can also be applied with this approach to intonation. Simply, have the students close their eyes while sustaining a pitch and visualize the speed of the beats and make the necessary adjustments until they can visualize a straight line.

Proceed to tuning octaves once you have established the above logical steps of unison tuning with your students. *This is the critical point in our instructional techniques. This is the point where students start to develop and experience auditory skills to the total ensemble sound, balance and blend through Vertical and Horizontal Sound Structure.*

Octave Tuning

Start with two students in a small group setting. If there are more than two students in the group, others will be listening for "beats." Change student "pairing" for unison and octave tuning. Always reinforce the *Logical Conclusions for Effective Intonation* given in the section on unison tuning.

Step #1

Student A will sustain either a low Bb concert or F concert (or other pitch which is most comfortable for the particular instrument) with a *MF* or *Forte* dynamic level. Student B will listen to Student A and then play the same pitch one octave higher at a *MP* level.

Step #2

Student B will play the octave above at a *mezzo piano* level while listening, *"become a part of the lower octave."* If beats occur, the horn needs adjustment relative to the Unison Tuning procedures outlined earlier. Adjust with the barrel or slide, it doesn't matter which direction, only that the "beats" slow down to the point where they are eliminated. The lower pitch must be the most prominent (Vertical Sound Structure).

Step #3

When the upper pitch becomes a *PART* of the lower octave and is not overly prominent, proper intonation, balance and blend has been achieved using the concept of Vertical Sound Structure (student B listens to the octave lower and adjusts volume for balance and blend with "beatless" tuning).

Step #4

As you proceed, add other students until you have the entire class or section responding to the logical conclusions of effective intonation. Have 2 students play the lower octave while the 3rd plays an octave higher. Then have 3 students play lower octave while 2 play the upper octave. Continue adding players, but always having more students on the lower pitch and fewer on the upper. When you have completed instruction in small group settings then apply and expect this tuning procedure with the entire organization.

This tuning procedure is most effective when you have processed your entire ensemble through small group settings. In a very short time you will recognize the improvement of intonation with your ensemble. The students will realize their importance and responsibility of intonation and *no longer will it be necessary for the director to go around the entire band and tune each student !* This type of situation only proves the directors ineffectiveness and inefficiency in dealing with intonation.

When you have instructed all students with unison and octave tuning, the next step will be to tune "beatless 5ths." This procedure follows the same concepts and *logical conclusions* as applied to unison and octave tuning.

Tuning the Interval of the 5th

Tuning the interval of the 5th is extremely important in the development of superior ensemble tone quality. It is at this point in which we alert and create effective student listening skills to *total ensemble sound, balance, blend and chord color.* Effective balance and blend is determined by the students auditory skills relative to the *fundamental.*

Step #1

Student A will play a "Bb" concert (or other pitch of your choosing). Student B will play an "F" concert after Student A plays and sustains the "Bb" concert.

Step #2

Student B will play the "5th" at a softer volume and listen for "beats." Student A should play the fundamental at a forte dynamic level. This is important because now you are also establishing the importance of inner parts and the foundation of superior ensemble sound.

Step #3

When the upper pitch *(5TH)* becomes a *PART* of the lower pitch *(fundamental),* and is not overly prominent and the two pitches are sounding "beatless," then proper intonation, balance and blend has been achieved using the concept of Vertical and Horizontal Sound Structure.

The principals and concepts of "Beatless Tuning" have been established in small group settings (lessons). Apply these same concepts in a full band rehearsal. In addition to these "beatless tuning" procedures, the students will follow the 3 logical steps defined for effective balance and blend found on the next page. *These 3 conditions are of critical importance in establishing student responsibility to the organizations overall sound quality.* Again, this approach removes the band director from tuning each individual player !

3 Logical Steps to Effective Balance & Blend

If you hear yourself above all others, 1 of 3 things is happening:

1. **You are overpowering or overblowing !** Make the necessary adjustment. *This initiates an auditory reaction to Balance.*

If you still hear yourself and you made the adjustment in #1, then:

2. **You are playing with poor tone quality !** Make the necessary adjustment (embouchure, breath support, posture, reed, etc.). *This initiates an auditory reaction to Blend* and a physical reaction to embouchure and breath support. Poor tone quality will not blend with anything !

If you still hear yourself and you made the adjustment in #1 and #2, then:

3. **You are playing out of tune !** Make the necessary adjustment by extending or shortening the length of your instrument. *This initiates an auditory reaction to "Beatless Tuning"* (see page 66 and continue with Intonation sequence).

The above steps are prioritized ! The relationships of these 3 steps is extremely important. One cannot come before the other. An instrument cannot be played in tune if overblowing or poor tone quality exists. This is the reason for tuning being the last step. The student must follow these in the correct order if improved ensemble sound is expected.

Tuning the Ensemble

Carefully review the graphic illustration on tuning procedures for the entire ensemble found on the following page. This approach and chart will assure you of a consistent pitch center within your organization. No longer will pitch discrepancies exist between woodwinds and brass or bass to soprano voices. The tuning procedure establishes "beatless" unisons and octaves in the entire organization.

The pitch starts with the tuba sustaining an F concert. This sustained F continues while building unisons and octaves up through the center of the band with all principal players. Do not have all principal players play at one time.

Principal Player Tuning

1. Tuba sustains F concert, point to the principal euphonium player to sound the octave F. The volume will be *less* than the tuba sound. The euphonium must become a *"part"* of the tuba sound.

2. When the tuba and euphonium have achieved *"beatless" octaves,* proceed with the 1st trombone. Tuba and euphonium will continue sounding the F concert, taking a breath when necessary.

3. Continue this process with all remaining principal players (see graphic illustration on following page). *As each player achieves "beatless" sound, the next principal player above comes in and builds upon all others to that point.* This process is followed all the way to the piccolo player.

4. When all principal players have achieved "beatless" octaves, stop and have the tuba sound F concert again and this time have the bassoons, and contra clarinets tune to the tuba.

5. Alto and Bari Saxophones tune both F and Bb Concert and compensate for the sharpness of F Concert. Use the same "Beatless" tuning procedures for Bb Concert.

Principal players tune first, starting from the Tuba and proceeding from bottom to top (center row of instruments).

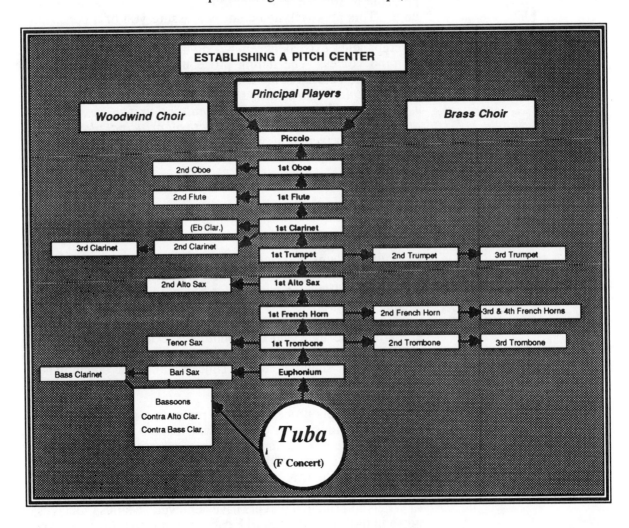

Continue with Section players after "Beatless" Unisons and Octaves have been established by all Principal Players.

Section Players Tune to Principals

Once all principal players have tuned unison and octaves, start with the Tuba again playing an F concert. Principal players will follow the same process, but this time *other section members will enter one at a time after their principal section leader enters.* Section players will use the 3 Logical Steps to Effective Balance and Blend (page 70).

The early stages will take more time but is well worth the effort when the students adapt to this tuning technique. In addition to tuning to F concert, other concert pitches should be used to better establish listening skills. It is important to sustain each pitch through the Circle of 4ths and apply concepts on pages 66 and 70.

Conclusion

By using the procedures outlined with *beatless tuning,* and starting with F concert, you will be successful in carrying these listening skills to other pitches. Once students are confident in listening for the "Speed of the Beats" and building pitch through Octaves and 5ths, a significant improvement will be recognized in the overall ensemble intonation and tone quality.

Review the concept and principals of tuning with the graphic illustration on page 72. It will assure you and your organization of a consistant pitch center. *Too often programs rely strictly on the Strobe for tuning (visual) and not the "ear for listening."* As I had stated earlier in this chapter, we have the most confidence in a "picture." The "strobe picture of tuning" creates security. Suspicion will always exist with what we hear because we neglect to visualize this sound. *Build your "ear" confidence by visualizing the "picture of intonation".....have the confidence and security of this "picture" that you hold in your "minds eye."*

Once the correct length of the instrument is achieved, the student must rely totally on his/her confidence to play in tune, especially when dealing with notes that must be compensated for. Therefore, it is important that this ear training take place and develop into a natural process for each student.

74

Chapter 5

Rhythmic Perception

Throughout this chapter, you will find techniques which will provide you with a logical approach in dealing with the measurement of sound and silence and its sub-divisions. Attention is directed to creating *"timed thinking"* (Internal Ensemble Pulse) with the total ensemble. The concepts and exercises are a means of developing a natural flow and response to rhythm. Moreover, developing *Internal Ensemble Pulse* through the *Measurement of Sound and Silence,* allows the director to create many unique approaches toward the organizations development of rhythmic perception. *It is a means of establishing rhythmic clarity and precision through Vertical and Horizontal Sound Structure by unifying and synchronizing mental pulse.*

Establishing Internal Ensemble Pulse is another essential aspect of superior performance ability. When *Internal Pulse is not* addressed through rehearsal procedures, a multitude of problems will arise throughout your performance. Such as: uneven flow and measurement of quarter, eighths, sixteenths; rushing or dragging rhythm patterns or syncopation; poor entrance and release; meter changes and transitions; or just a generally cluttered, undefined, distorted sound; to name a few.

A tremendous amount of rehearsal time is consumed with repetitive exercises to achieve clarity and definition of notated rhythms. The difficulty lies in how we, as directors, create an awareness and mental response to an *""unseen division of space." The problem does not lie with the individual's reaction to note values, but in the techniques we used to establish this unification or synchronization of sub-divided "space" and its duration within the entire organization.* It is more than repetition, and more than having a group of individuals play rhythmic exercises from a method book. The ensemble's rhythmic perception must be addressed through the development of the students mental, spatial (not dealing with objects but perception of melodic content as a whole) and kinesthetic response relative to other band members.

Sound, through inner (mental) pulse, must be aligned vertically and horizontally to achieve perfection. This alignment has to do with how students perceive tempo and pulse. To achieve the motion and momentum of music, we must be sensitive to a sub-divided pulse. When such an inner ensemble pulse is achieved, the director is then able to move this pulse forward or back (accelerando and ritardando) with a unified feeling from all individuals. This allows the conductor to achieve greater freedom in expression instead of a contrived expression through repetition.

Method books, with a multitude of approaches, deal with this performance technique strictly through the repetitious reading of rhythmic exercises written for individual or large ensembles. *Such an approach does not address or stress what is "happening" internally or mentally, or what is being perceived by the individual student relative to the total ensemble.* By creating exercises through visual imagery, we can better activate the mind and auditory senses relative to the measurement of sound and silence. Internal Ensemble Pulse is achieved through the unification or synchronization of "mental" time. In creating this perception of time and rhythm, it is important that the concept of Vertical and Horizontal sound structure be maintained.

Sound in music is "life." "Life" moves forward.......we cannot go back or stand still in time........music must create the same feeling of "life." Music must have direction and motion. *Its motion is created by the internal energy which the performer generates cooperatively with other members. The mechanical activity is insignificant to the expression of music making !*

The most significant aspect of this teaching technique in establishing this awareness of tempo, pulse, and its sub-divisions is that the conductor no longer *""beats time"* for the organization. *The organization "senses" and "feels" one unified pulse which every individual relies upon through a relaxed, confident state of awareness.*

When applying these concepts and exercises, the director must focus his attention and awareness to the organizations ability to concentrate "in time" and, how long the concentration is controlled !

Hasty judgements should not be made during the early stages. The first experiences in unifying this mental pulse of time will only be 10 -20 seconds or less. If the first try is 10 seconds, then the second and third attempts increase to 25-35 seconds. You must be aware of this and extend with each subsequent rehearsal.

This awareness is essential for the director. *The ultimate goal is total concentration for the entire length of a particular composition* (which could be 20 minutes in length with a major composition).

Proceed with the following concepts and techniques to unify internal mental pulse.

Measurement of Sound and Silence

The most neglected area in our instructional program is the measurement of silence and what happens during this time. *The reason for such neglect is, we, as music teachers, do not have a planned course of action to deal with silence.* More often than not, the students are instructed only to count the number of beats and then make their entrance. Moreover, if a student is playing a selection in his/her lesson, and a section has several measures of rests, the teacher reaction will often be, "O.K. let's continue and not count out the rests at this time." This is a natural reaction for expediency and efficiency in a lesson setting (no one questions this approach). We *assume* the student is capable of counting "x" number of beats and can maintain the pulse. This approach is *uncontrolled thinking* and in no way develops a disciplined technique to *silence*. Without silence, there is no melody or rhythm, and loud and soft gain their meaning in reference to silence.

Entrance and Release

The superior band program always performs with exactness, clarity and definition. The directors of such programs have developed teaching techniques to acquire such accuracy. This type of performance skill is determined by the organizations ability to maintain a *Silent Internal Ensemble Pulse !*

The effectiveness of ENTRANCE is determined by the organizations ability to visually react to the directors preparatory beat and to internally maintain this pulse. The imperfections will come from those individuals who do not have this synchronized or unified sense of timing. The exercises written will develop a synchronized-unified-internal pulse within the students; including an awareness to the "whole" ensemble sound and where they are relative to this "whole."

The effectiveness of RELEASE is determined by the organizations ability to fulfill the demands of DURATION while maintaining a unified internal ensemble pulse. Any individual negligence in this area of musical performance plays "havoc" on musical quality. I might add, a conceptual conflict arises when we address the *release* of a note, as the *"end."* *Music is sound moving forward; it doesn't stop until the last note has disappeared into SILENCE.* If we approach the *release* as the *beginning of silence,* a totally different sensory reaction becomes apparent. *It is not how a note ENDS, but how SILENCE BEGINS,* is what really must be addressed. Therefore, the *silence* which follows any *release,* or the very last note of a composition, now takes on new meaning ! Such a concept retains the motion of music. It addresses the release of a note into (and) silence simultaneously. This has greater significance to an artistic expression.

In developing and establishing a unified mental pulse with *entrance* and *release,* in a wholistic concept, it is important that *odd number combinations* be used. The students are very capable and comfortable with sensing 2's and 4's. By changing and using odd numbers, we begin and control the students thinking process. Such combinations will change many bad habits developed through common time signatures. This rehearsal technique is significant in achieving total control and attention to the smallest detail.

Odd Numbers

Inform the students that it is extremely important that total silence be maintained when the entire ensemble is *"sensing"* and mentally counting *"SILENCE."* Any type of noise will distract the students intensity of concentration. If

noise will distract the students intensity of concentration. If such a condition arises (movement, chair squeeking, class bells ringing), stop and wait until total silence is restored and then proceed....*with a different odd number combination ! These different combinations are what controls "thinking."*

Using the Circle of 4ths and using odd number combinations of sound and silence, have students play the pitches in unison and octaves (or assign each group their pitch for Major chords). The directions given will be as follows:

Example.....Sustain SOUND for 7 beats, followed by 5 beats of SILENCE. Continue this throughout the Circle of 4ths.

"As you are sustaining the sound for 7 beats, count mentally from 1 thru 7....... the moment your mind thinks of 7, RELEASE into SILENCE...... followed by silently saying, REST 2, 3, 4, 5 (in tempo)....then proceed to the next pitch in the Circle (in tempo)..... the next pitch ENTRANCE will START the moment your mind thinks of "1" and continue the process throughout the Circle.

This procedure is followed for all number combinations. It is important that students say the word "rest" when starting silence." The word "rest" only controls the students thinking. The number combinations should not be related to any type of note value. You will address note values only in literature preparation (whole note is actually a release on 5, or dotted half is a release on 4, etc.).

SOUND should be given an odd number value and the *SILENCE* that follows should have a different odd number value. As the ensemble's precision improves, the odd numbers for silence will increase. *The ensemble with outstanding Internal Pulse is one that can control the longest measured SILENCE with the most precise ENTRANCE on a Vertical and Horizontal basis.*

You will establish a pulse (counting or tapping aloud) for the students to sense. *Start the ensemble and count aloud during the first 2 or 3 pitches they are sustaining and for the SILENCE part, say "REST 2,3,4,5,etc." This is important in unifying the mental pulse.*

At this point, stop counting and step away form the podium. Allow the students to continue throughout the Circle of 4ths on their own. When you detect a poor entrance or release, stop the organization and START OVER WITH A NEW COMBINATION OF NUMBERS. Do this 2 or 3 times and concentration increases significantly. The students become aware and "hear" the imperfection and by starting over, the concentration intensifies. It is not the playing exercise that is important....the priority is the command of the unified thinking process. Remember to *step away and DO NOT CONDUCT after the first 2 or 3 sound and silence combinations* (refer to Chapter 7).

This rehearsal technique, when used for a brief time at the beginning of each rehearsal, will significantly improve your ensemble *(this is a guarantee).* Be sensitive to the students attention and improved listening, especially when you follow with the regular literature being rehearsed and start addressing entrances and releases.

The essential aspect of this teaching technique is that every student WILL COUNT (and in the pulse the director has established) to achieve accuracy with entrance and release. *The students sensory reaction is focused on duration (Horizontal Sound Structure), with a group sensitivity to total ensemble pulse (Vertical Sound Structure).*

On the following page is a graphic illustration of Sound and Silence exercises.

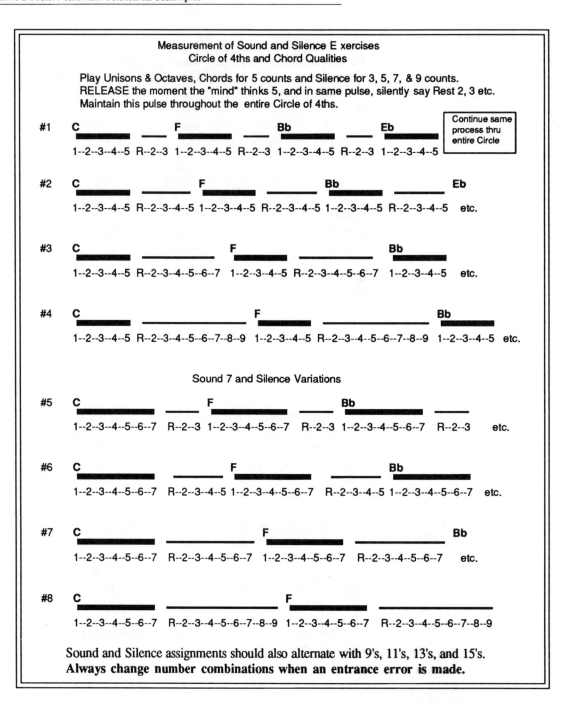

Measurement of Sound and Silence E xercises
Circle of 4ths and Chord Qualities

Play Unisons & Octaves, Chords for 5 counts and Silence for 3, 5, 7, & 9 counts.
RELEASE the moment the "mind" thinks 5, and in same pulse, silently say Rest 2, 3 etc.
Maintain this pulse throughout the entire Circle of 4ths.

Continue same process thru entire Circle

#1 C   F   Bb   Eb
1--2--3--4--5 R--2--3 1--2--3--4--5 R--2--3 1--2--3--4--5 R--2--3 1--2--3--4--5

#2 C   F   Bb   Eb
1--2--3--4--5 R--2--3--4--5 1--2--3--4--5 R--2--3--4--5 1--2--3--4--5 R--2--3--4--5   etc.

#3 C   F   Bb
1--2--3--4--5 R--2--3--4--5--6--7 1--2--3--4--5 R--2--3--4--5--6--7 1--2--3--4--5   etc.

#4 C   F   Bb
1--2--3--4--5 R--2--3--4--5--6--7--8--9 1--2--3--4--5 R--2--3--4--5--6--7--8--9 1--2--3--4--5   etc.

Sound 7 and Silence Variations

#5 C   F   Bb
1--2--3--4--5--6--7 R--2--3 1--2--3--4--5--6--7 R--2--3 1--2--3--4--5--6--7 R--2--3   etc.

#6 C   F   Bb
1--2--3--4--5--6--7 R--2--3--4--5 1--2--3--4--5--6--7 R--2--3--4--5 1--2--3--4--5--6--7   etc.

#7 C   F   Bb
1--2--3--4--5--6--7 R--2--3--4--5--6--7 1--2--3--4--5--6--7 R--2--3--4--5--6--7   etc.

#8 C   F
1--2--3--4--5--6--7 R--2--3--4--5--6--7--8--9 1--2--3--4--5--6--7 R--2--3--4--5--6--7--8--9

Sound and Silence assignments should also alternate with 9's, 11's, 13's, and 15's.
Always change number combinations when an entrance error is made.

Other exercises below are used to create variations to each rehearsal or when this concept is being stressed. Please note that the duration of Sound is *NEVER* the same as the duration of *SILENCE*. Do not stay with any Variation, change frequently between 3's, 5's, 7's, etc.

Variations on 3's			Variations on 5's	
Sound	Silence		Sound	Silence
3	5		5	3
3	7		5	7
3	9		5	9
3	11		5	11
3	13		5	13
3	15		5	15

Variations on 7's			Variations on 9's	
Sound	Silence		Sound	Silence
7	3		9	3
7	5		9	5
7	9		9	7
7	11		9	11
7	13		9	13
7	15		9	15

The above odd number combination are only to make you aware of the unlimited number combinations possible. Each daily warm-up is different, but still achieves the goal of developing a unified Internal Ensemble Pulse. *It is extremely important that no type of pattern or day to day habit be formed with these exercises. They will be changed constantly for each rehearsal and when an error is made with Entrance or Release by an individual or section. Continue to reinforce Horizontal and Vertical Sound Structure throughout these exercises.*

Use any type of chord quality, unisons, or rhythm pattern. The important aspects of these exercises is to extend the interval of silence with *absolute "timed" mental control. The longer the interval of silence, with the most precise entrance, reflects an organization which has unified their internal feeling of pulse.....the highest numbers for silence are the most demanding for concentration !*

It is also critical that total silence (no foot tapping, body movement, whispering or any type of noise) be maintained when students are internally pulsing silence. The least little noise is a distraction to sensitivity and the concentration process which we are establishing with this teaching technique. *To further intensify concentration, have students close their eyes when doing Sound and Silence exercises* (refer to Chapter 3, *Creating an Aural and Visual Image of Sound*).

What you will experience in the first rehearsal:

1. Don't become *alarmed* because of a total collapse during the first 10-20 seconds. *The students are not accustomed to such a teaching technique. It demands "thinking."* Don't overreact; stop and proceed with different odd number combinations. Be aware of student concentration; has it *increased* or *decreased ?* This is determined by the length of time the entire band can control this thinking process before "breaking down." When it breaks down after the second or third try, move to other material. *Change patterns for the next days rehearsal.... it's not the exercise , it's the mental process.*

2. Students who have poor thinking habits will be the first to become frustrated. Don't give up, *they have never been expected to use their thinking skills in this manner.* Have patience and encourage these individuals. *It is usually the teacher who cannot cope with this type of situation because there is a feeling of "wasting time." We are dealing with extremely subtle awareness techniques.*

3. You will discover how poor (or superior) *entrance* and *releases* are played. The poor *entrance* and *release* will be addressed through Vertical and Horizontal sound structure. If your organization is superior, you will now be able to address still a finer degree or detail to this area.

4. By not conducting these exercises (only in the opening segments) you and your students become extremely aware of *"time." A more intense form of concentration and pulse is developed between director and students.* (Refer to Chapter 8).

5. As you proceed with this technique you will find less talking, whispering, movement, and daydreaming. Rehearsal intensity and momentum increases significantly.

6. A significant improvement in musical performance will be quite apparent as you continue to develop more complex musical expectations.*You will have "broken through the barrier" into the actual control and direction of the students thought process.*

7. Don't overreact, but be patient. Work with this approach for at least a month and you will be convinced. *A totally new direction in rehearsal techniques will be developing for you.*

Impatience will be your biggest enemy. Moreover, as the techniques develop, you and your organization will be functioning with maximum productivity. Your unlimited potential will become evident and the day to day "habits of boredom" will disappear.

The entire concept and method develops combined mental intensity of both students and conductor !

Rhythm Patterns

When the ensemble has an understanding of sustaining and measuring sound and silence with Chord Qualities around the Circle of 4ths, proceed and vary the day to day rehearsals with rhythm patterns. The same principals apply to rhythm patterns as were stated in the section dealing with sound and silence. The application of rhythm patterns is the next level in the development of a *Unified Internal Ensemble Pulse.*

Rhythm patterns have unlimited approaches with this system of rehearsal techniques. I have included a few of the variations. Some are very basic while others are more complex patterns. Review the exercises and develop your own for your specific ensemble needs. Isolate some of the more demanding rhythm patterns found in the literature you are preparing and use them throughout the Circle of 4ths. You will quickly recognize the unlimited approaches that will take the students through all keys in the Circle of 4ths.

Examples:

     1. Rhythms dealing with odd numbers, followed by silence.

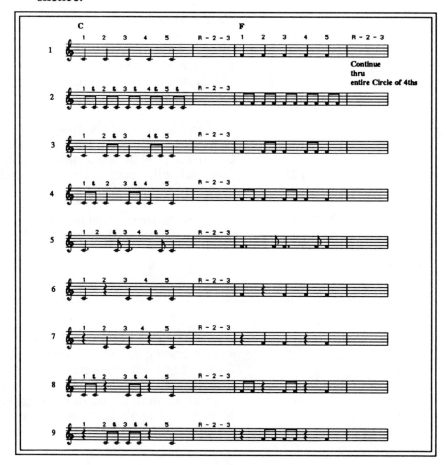

86

2.   Brass playing one rhythm while woodwinds play another.

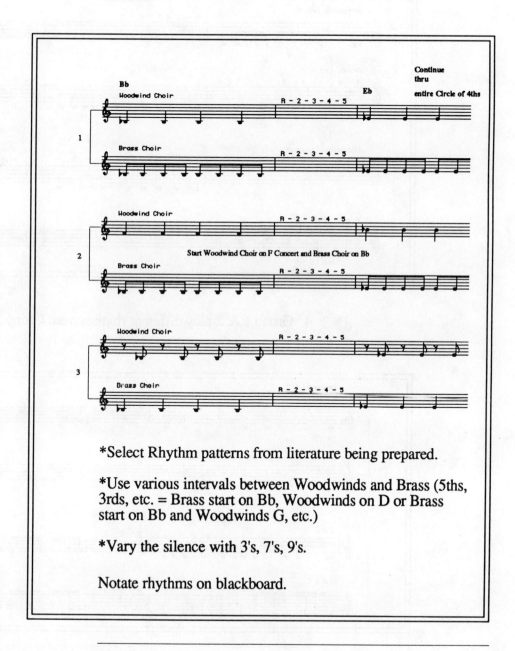

*Select Rhythm patterns from literature being prepared.

*Use various intervals between Woodwinds and Brass (5ths, 3rds, etc. = Brass start on Bb, Woodwinds on D or Brass start on Bb and Woodwinds G, etc.)

*Vary the silence with 3's, 7's, 9's.

Notate rhythms on blackboard.

3. Brass play one rhythm and alternate with woodwinds.

4. Group 1 & 2 play different rhythm from Group 3 & 4.

5. Mixed meters such as 5/8,7/8,10/8, etc.

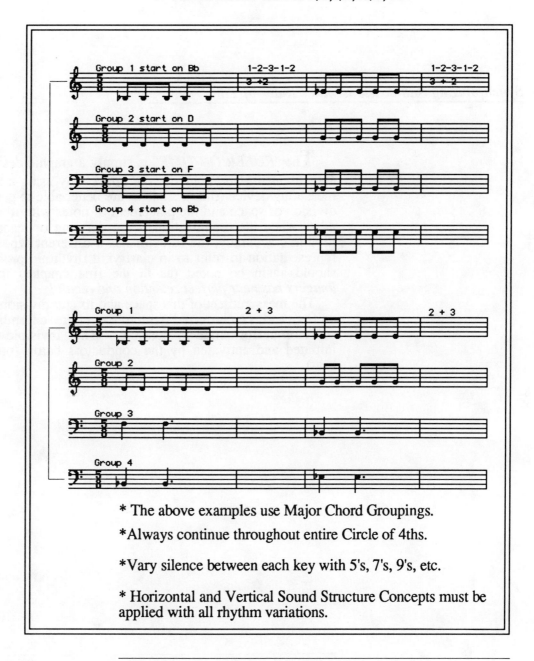

* The above examples use Major Chord Groupings.

*Always continue throughout entire Circle of 4ths.

*Vary silence between each key with 5's, 7's, 9's, etc.

* Horizontal and Vertical Sound Structure Concepts must be applied with all rhythm variations.

Synchronizing Sub-divisions with "Ruler of Time"

The *"RULER OF TIME"* is simply a graphic design of the *Measurement and Subdivision of Space*. By using a traditional measuring device (ruler), students are better able to perceive the division of space and the placement of notes within this space. Also, when the organization is not defining or responding to rhythmic accuracy, the director has a different type of visual representation to refer to in clarifying rhythmic problems. It should again be noted (as in the first chapter) that *visual imagery has near perfect retention and recall !*

The measurement of this space and its sub-divisions must be unified and synchronized within the entire ensemble before superior performance is possible. This Invisible Space is initiated and activated by the conductors baton (preparatory beat).

Ruler of Time

The length and width of the "Ruler of Time" is determined by tempo !

The lower and upper Horizontal lines are the "invisible lines" which represent the "down" and "up" beat of the conductors baton.

The 3 Horizontal lines found between the upper and lower lines are the sub-divisions of "space" between beats (16ths & 32nds).

The slower the TEMPO, the longer and wider "space" of sub-divisions.

The faster the TEMPO, the shorter and narrower "space" of sub-divisions.

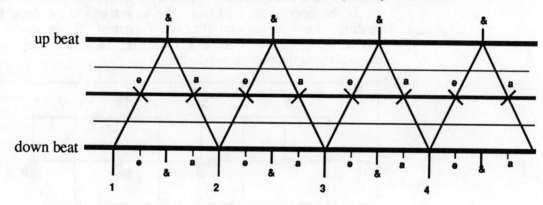

The Measurement of this "SPACE" is activated by the conductors baton (prep beat).

The Measurement of this "SPACE" and its sub-divisions must be SYNCHRONIZED within the entire Ensemble for rhythmic accuracy and clarity.

This graphic design allows the student to create a visual awareness to the *"exactness"* or *"precision"* of their rhythmic reaction. By creating such a teaching technique, the students can first *"SEE"* (very much the same as tuning to a Stroboconn) and then *"LISTEN."* This provides an additional sensory response and significantly improves the listening skill.

Applying in Rehearsal or Lesson:

1. Make a large chart of the *"RULER OF TIME"* and position it in an appropriate place where all students can view, or draw the "ruler" on a blackboard.

2. Any type of rhythm the students are having problems with can easily be placed in its proper spacing on the "ruler."

3. Inaccuracies can be approached on the "Ruler" with a *TARGET*. Example: If students are not reacting to after beats, describe how the *TARGET* is precisely where the point of "&" meets the upper line. Missing the target would be done by placing "dots" before and after the Target of "&" in showing this to the students. Each dot would represent a student not responding at the precise subdivision.

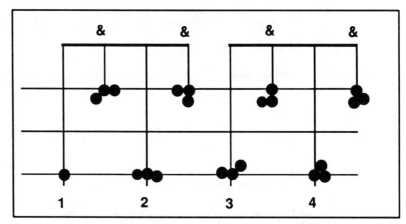

4. During a rehearsal, the director should use his music stand as the lower horizontal line and hold a pencil with his left hand above and parallel to the lower line or stand. Instruct students to play when your baton **taps** the stand on the *"DOWN"* beat, and when the baton **taps** the pencil at the *"UP"* beat.

5. When students are reacting to #4 (above), then have them only play on the *"UP"* beat the moment the baton "taps" the pencil held in your left hand. Be sure to "tap" the stand on the *"DOWN"* beat.

6. Explain the concept of "space" between the lower line (stand) and the upper line (pencil or other-blackboard). This "space" is determined by tempo...... the greater width is *Slow* tempo and subdivision; the narrower width is *Faster* tempo and sub-divisions.

7. Have students play a note on the *"Down"* beats at slow and fast tempo's. Then have students play notes on the *"Up"* beats at slow and fast tempo's. Always use the two horizontal lines ("down" and "up" beat) in establishing this concept. This technique creates *immediate visual* and *auditory* reaction.

At the conclusion of this Method, I have included a variety of rhythm patterns drawn to scale and can be placed over the "Ruler of Time." Simply, make overhead transparencies of the "Ruler of Time" and rhythm patterns. Periodically in rehearsal use an overhead projector and place transparencies of rhythm patterns over the Ruler. The students will quickly recognize the correct placement of notes in their sub-divided position and realize the importance of *Internal Ensemble Pulse*. You should also use the "Ruler" and make transparencies of complex rhythms found in the literature you are preparing with your organization.

Compressing Measures

Quite often organizations with poor rhythmic perception and uneven Internal Ensemble Pulse, will make measures shorter or smaller relative to previous measures. *This poor rhythmic sense always will lead to Sections or individuals "arriving" at a Beat before it happens.* This creates a distorted, undefined sound on a Vertical structure because sections or individuals do not "line up" or unify the Internal Ensemble pulse (the same description is also true for Horizontal Sound Structure).

For this type of musical performance deficiency, I often refer to this as *compressing measures*. It is directly related to Internal Ensemble Pulse and the groups sensitivity to Horizontal and Vertical Sound Structure. In addition to compressing measures (space), measures can also be lengthened. Students or sections would play slightly longer note values and sub-divisions and not "arrive" at the exact placement of the sub-divided beat.

The illustration below, visually represents such misalignment of sub-divisions creating *compressed measures*.

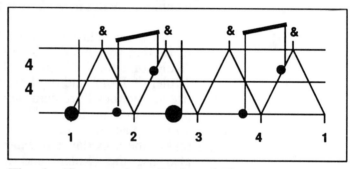

The significance of the "Ruler of Time" is the director can visually display the organizational deficiencies and have a means or technique for correction and improvement. *Compressing measures* creates a new concept in dealing with such ensemble problems. It provides the director with a different avenue of techniques to achieve the clarity and definition needed.

Listen carefully for *compressed measures* when applying the "Ruler" concept with the rhythmic variations from simple to complex.

Conclusion

Throughout this chapter, sufficient amount of rehearsal material has been presented to assist you in developing greater sensitivity and awareness to rhythmic perception. Its design and intent is to remove the boring day to day approaches of insignificant rhythmic practice and repetition. Review the concepts and methods periodically. Your own unique techniques will evolve while applying those outlined.

Chapter 6

Dynamics

This chapter deals with instructional techniques in the development of *Crescendos, Decrescendos, Sforzando's,* and *"FP" entrances.* The teaching techniques are integrated and consistent with other techniques presented. They provide the director with reference points when dealing with dynamic contrast. When used with Chord Qualities around the Circle of 4ths, you will have an effective technique to "tailor" the total ensemble sound to your liking. The most significant aspect of this approach is the ease and positive results obtained when dealing with *balance, blend, tone quality* and *chord color* at various dynamic levels. Students quickly recognize and *hear* what happens when all sections and individuals respond with equal effort.

Graphic illustrations are used so that, students can create a mental picture of expanding and contracting sound. Numbers are used in dynamic variations similar to the *"Sound and Silence"* exercises. They serve a dual purpose when used with dynamic variations. *The approach continues to strengthen the students "unified internal ensemble pulse" while focusing attention to the volume of sound, relative to the number value. The "number" technique is simply a reference point and a means to communicate the variations of volume.* Simply, "the lesser the number, the lesser the volume,......the greater the number the greater the volume." Therefore, "1" can be assigned a dynamic level of *"PPP"* or *"PP"* and a 5, 7, 9, or 11 can be assigned a *"Forte"* or *"Fortissimo"* level.

Instruct the students to mentally count from 1 to 5 (or 7,9,11) while playing a *Crescendo* and counting in reverse from 5 (or 7, 9, 11) to 1 while playing a *Decrescendo. They will expand the sound as they mentally count to the higher number and decrease as they mentally count in reverse to 1.* With these number relationships, it is quite difficult *not* to respond. The student has a clear and specific direction regarding the goal. Volume which is designated at a "5" level will always be greater than "3" or "4" relative to our natural reaction to number values.

This concept effectively establishes a greater response and sensitivity to the expected dynamic contrast. The approach assures that every student will increase or decrease the volume of sound being made.

The following graphic illustrations and examples are done in sequential order. *The introductory approaches are done in a very mechanical fashion and attention is directed to the "mind" counting through the numbers forward and reverse while projecting the volume of sound implied by the number.* This process will become very comfortable. In a very short period of time, the *"total ensemble ear"* will react to *balance, blend,* and *chord color* while increasing or decreasing sound.

The exercises in dynamics should not be presented until your organization has established a clear understanding of Vertical and Horizontal Sound Structure along with Chord Color (refer to Chapter 3).

During the introductory stages, the director is only to make a very small downward pulse with the baton. Do not imply any type of crescendo or decrescendo with the left hand.... rely on the students mentally counting through the numbers for the expansion and contraction of volume. Once you have gone beyond these initial stages, you will be free to move throughout the band or step to the side and focus all your attention to *balance, blend, tone quality,* and *chord color.* This procedure removes the director from "beating time," or implying the dynamics with hand movements. *It shifts the responsibility to the students ability to listen and function within the total ensemble sound.*

Many of dynamic variations have been written using a number sequence from "1" to "5." They should be expanded to "7, 9, and 11" including variations with *F's, FF's, MF's, etc.* The exercises which include "silence" should also be changed from the indicated "3," to 5 and 7's.

The dynamic examples can be duplicated and distributed to each student if necessary. The many variations illustrated are only intended to show the director the unlimited possibilities with this teaching technique. Review them carefully, especially pages 101 - 105. These exercises deal with alternating choirs and the numerical assignments are important for success. Page 106 will create (Percy Grainger, contrary dynamics) some very interesting dynamic effects. Use these exercises once students become comfortable with the previous variations. *All exercises will be used with the Circle of 4ths with unisons, octaves and chord qualities.*

Full Ensemble Decrescendo Exercises

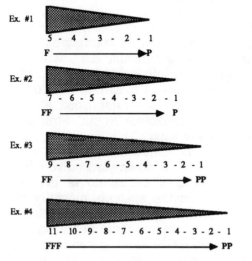

Instruct students to mentally count all numbers in reverse as they sustain and diminish sound (as the numbers decrease, so does the volume).

Use the Circle of 4ths in unison and octaves. As the students become acquainted with the relationships of numbers and volume, then use Major and Minor Chord quality groupings.

Full Ensemble Crescendo

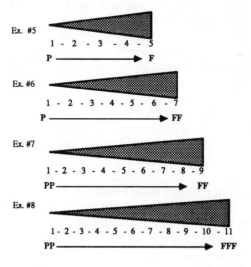

Instruct students to mentally count all numbers and increase volume as they mentally count to the highest number

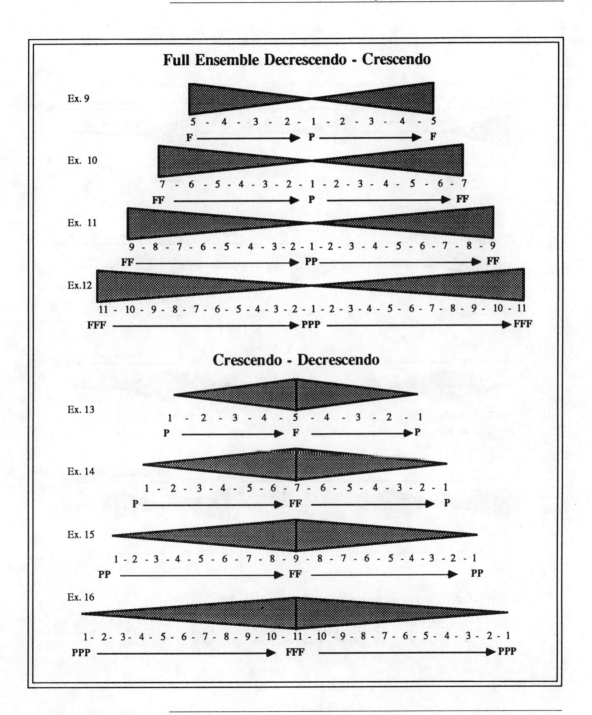

Full Ensemble Decrescendo - Crescendo

Ex. 9

5 - 4 - 3 - 2 - 1 - 2 - 3 - 4 - 5
F ─────────────► P ─────────────► F

Ex. 10

7 - 6 - 5 - 4 - 3 - 2 - 1 - 2 - 3 - 4 - 5 - 6 - 7
FF ─────────────► P ─────────────► FF

Ex. 11

9 - 8 - 7 - 6 - 5 - 4 - 3 - 2 - 1 - 2 - 3 - 4 - 5 - 6 - 7 - 8 - 9
FF ─────────────► PP ─────────────► FF

Ex. 12

11 - 10 - 9 - 8 - 7 - 6 - 5 - 4 - 3 - 2 - 1 - 2 - 3 - 4 - 5 - 6 - 7 - 8 - 9 - 10 - 11
FFF ─────────────► PPP ─────────────► FFF

Crescendo - Decrescendo

Ex. 13

1 - 2 - 3 - 4 - 5 - 4 - 3 - 2 - 1
P ─────────────► F ─────────────► P

Ex. 14

1 - 2 - 3 - 4 - 5 - 6 - 7 - 6 - 5 - 4 - 3 - 2 - 1
P ─────────────► FF ─────────────► P

Ex. 15

1 - 2 - 3 - 4 - 5 - 6 - 7 - 8 - 9 - 8 - 7 - 6 - 5 - 4 - 3 - 2 - 1
PP ─────────────► FF ─────────────► PP

Ex. 16

1 - 2 - 3 - 4 - 5 - 6 - 7 - 8 - 9 - 10 - 11 - 10 - 9 - 8 - 7 - 6 - 5 - 4 - 3 - 2 - 1
PPP ─────────────► FFF ─────────────► PPP

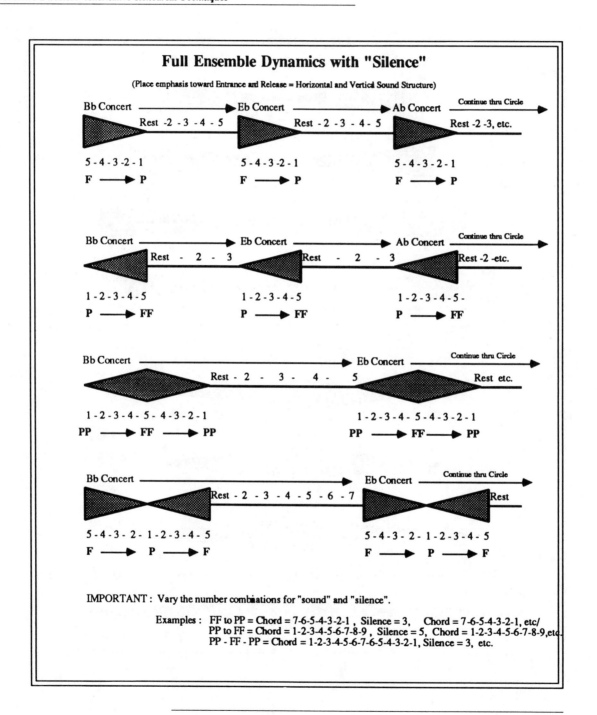

Full Ensemble Dynamics with "Silence"

(Place emphasis toward Entrance and Release = Horizontal and Vertical Sound Structure)

IMPORTANT : Vary the number combinations for "sound" and "silence".

Examples : FF to PP = Chord = 7-6-5-4-3-2-1 , Silence = 3,   Chord = 7-6-5-4-3-2-1, etc/
PP to FF = Chord = 1-2-3-4-5-6-7-8-9 , Silence = 5, Chord = 1-2-3-4-5-6-7-8-9,etc.
PP - FF - PP = Chord = 1-2-3-4-5-6-7-6-5-4-3-2-1, Silence = 3, etc.

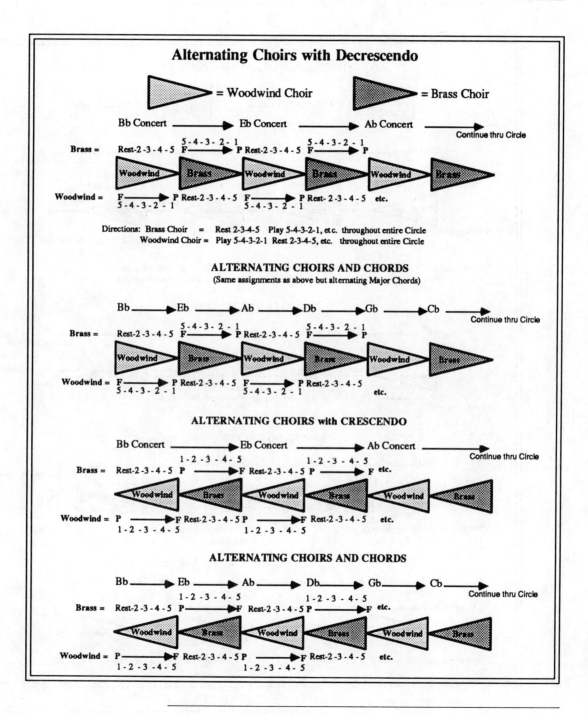

Alternating Choirs with Decrescendo

⬛ = Woodwind Choir   ⬛ = Brass Choir

Bb Concert ⟶ Eb Concert ⟶ Ab Concert ⟶ Continue thru Circle

Brass = Rest-2 -3 - 4 - 5 F⟶P Rest-2 -3 - 4 - 5 F⟶P
                    5 - 4 - 3 - 2 - 1   5 - 4 - 3 - 2 - 1

Woodwind | Brass | Woodwind | Brass | Woodwind | Brass

Woodwind = F⟶P Rest- 2 -3 - 4 - 5 F⟶P Rest- 2 -3 - 4 - 5 etc.
                5 - 4 - 3 - 2 - 1   5 - 4 - 3 - 2 - 1

Directions: Brass Choir   =   Rest 2-3-4-5 Play 5-4-3-2-1, et c. throughout entire Circle
            Woodwind Choir =   Play 5-4-3-2-1 Rest 2-3-4-5, etc.   throughout entire Circle

ALTERNATING CHOIRS AND CHORDS
(Same assignments as above but alternating Major Chords)

Bb ⟶ Eb ⟶ Ab ⟶ Db ⟶ Gb ⟶ Cb ⟶ Continue thru Circle

Brass = Rest-2 -3 - 4 - 5 F⟶P Rest-2 -3 - 4 - 5 F⟶P
                    5 - 4 - 3 - 2 - 1   5 - 4 - 3 - 2 - 1

Woodwind | Brass | Woodwind | Brass | Woodwind | Brass

Woodwind = F⟶P Rest-2 -3 - 4 - 5 F⟶P Rest-2 -3 - 4 - 5
                5 - 4 - 3 - 2 - 1   5 - 4 - 3 - 2 - 1   etc.

ALTERNATING CHOIRS with CRESCENDO

Bb Concert ⟶ Eb Concert ⟶ Ab Concert ⟶ Continue thru Circle

Brass = Rest-2 -3 - 4 - 5 P⟶F Rest-2 -3 - 4 - 5 P⟶F etc.
                    1 - 2 - 3 - 4 - 5   1 - 2 - 3 - 4 - 5

Woodwind | Brass | Woodwind | Brass | Woodwind | Brass

Woodwind = P⟶F Rest-2 - 3 - 4 - 5 P⟶F Rest-2 - 3 - 4 - 5 etc.
                1 - 2 - 3 - 4 - 5   1 - 2 - 3 - 4 - 5

ALTERNATING CHOIRS AND CHORDS

Bb ⟶ Eb ⟶ Ab ⟶ Db ⟶ Gb ⟶ Cb ⟶ Continue thru Circle

Brass = Rest-2 -3 - 4 - 5 P⟶F Rest-2 -3 - 4 - 5 P⟶F etc.
                    1 - 2 - 3 - 4 - 5   1 - 2 - 3 - 4 - 5

Woodwind | Brass | Woodwind | Brass | Woodwind | Brass

Woodwind = P⟶F Rest-2 - 3 - 4 - 5 P⟶F Rest-2 - 3 - 4 - 5 etc.
                1 - 2 - 3 - 4 - 5   1 - 2 - 3 - 4 - 5

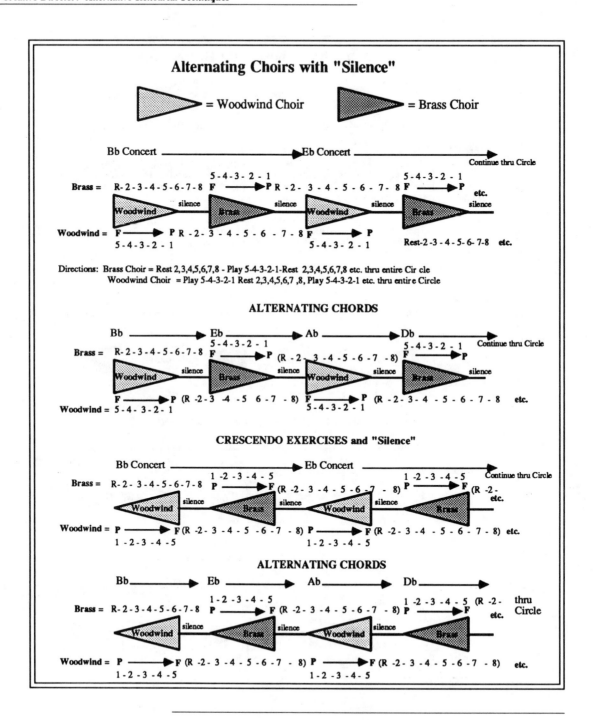

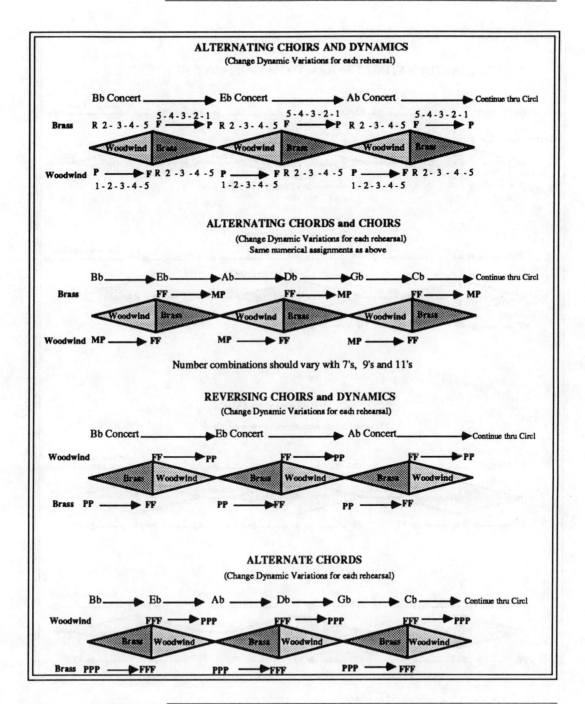

ALTERNATING CHOIRS AND DYNAMICS
(Change Dynamic Variations for each rehearsal)

Bb Concert ⟶ Eb Concert ⟶ Ab Concert ⟶ Continue thru Circl

Brass   R 2 - 3 - 4 - 5 F ⟶ P   R 2 - 3 - 4 - 5 F ⟶ P   R 2 - 3 - 4 - 5 F ⟶ P

5 - 4 - 3 - 2 - 1   5 - 4 - 3 - 2 - 1   5 - 4 - 3 - 2 - 1

Woodwind Woodwind Brass   Woodwind Brass   Woodwind Brass

Woodwind P ⟶ F R 2 - 3 - 4 - 5   P ⟶ F R 2 - 3 - 4 - 5   P ⟶ F R 2 - 3 - 4 - 5

1 - 2 - 3 - 4 - 5   1 - 2 - 3 - 4 - 5   1 - 2 - 3 - 4 - 5

ALTERNATING CHORDS and CHOIRS
(Change Dynamic Variations for each rehearsal)
Same numerical assignments as above

Bb ⟶ Eb ⟶ Ab ⟶ Db ⟶ Gb ⟶ Cb ⟶ Continue thru Circl

Brass   FF ⟶ MP   FF ⟶ MP   FF ⟶ MP

Woodwind Brass   Woodwind Brass   Woodwind Brass

Woodwind MP ⟶ FF   MP ⟶ FF   MP ⟶ FF

Number combinations should vary with 7's, 9's and 11's

REVERSING CHOIRS and DYNAMICS
(Change Dynamic Variations for each rehearsal)

Bb Concert ⟶ Eb Concert ⟶ Ab Concert ⟶ Continue thru Circl

Woodwind   FF ⟶ PP   FF ⟶ PP   FF ⟶ PP

Brass Woodwind   Brass Woodwind   Brass Woodwind

Brass PP ⟶ FF   PP ⟶ FF   PP ⟶ FF

ALTERNATE CHORDS
(Change Dynamic Variations for each rehearsal)

Bb ⟶ Eb ⟶ Ab ⟶ Db ⟶ Gb ⟶ Cb ⟶ Continue thru Circl

Woodwind   FFF ⟶ PPP   FFF ⟶ PPP   FFF ⟶ PPP

Brass Woodwind   Brass Woodwind   Brass Woodwind

Brass PPP ⟶ FFF   PPP ⟶ FFF   PPP ⟶ FFF

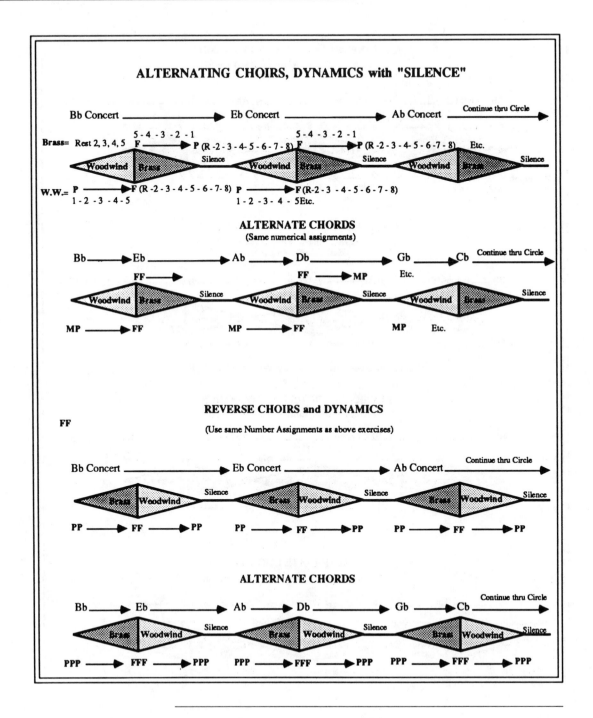

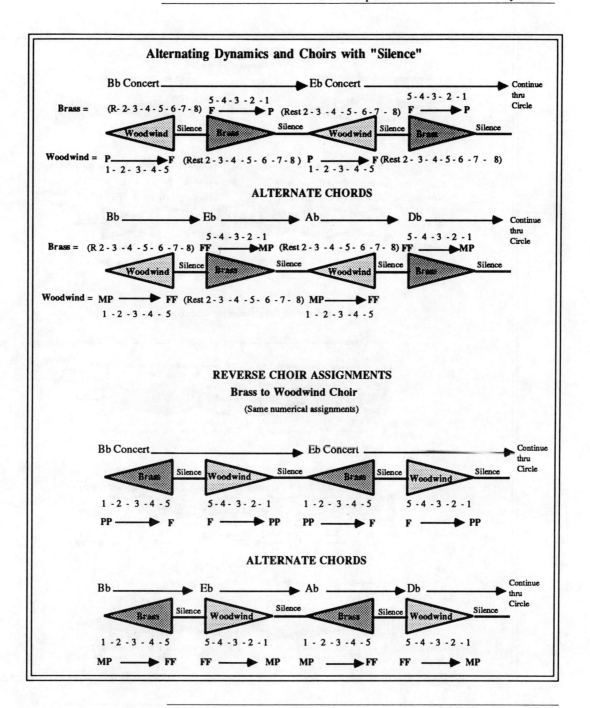

105

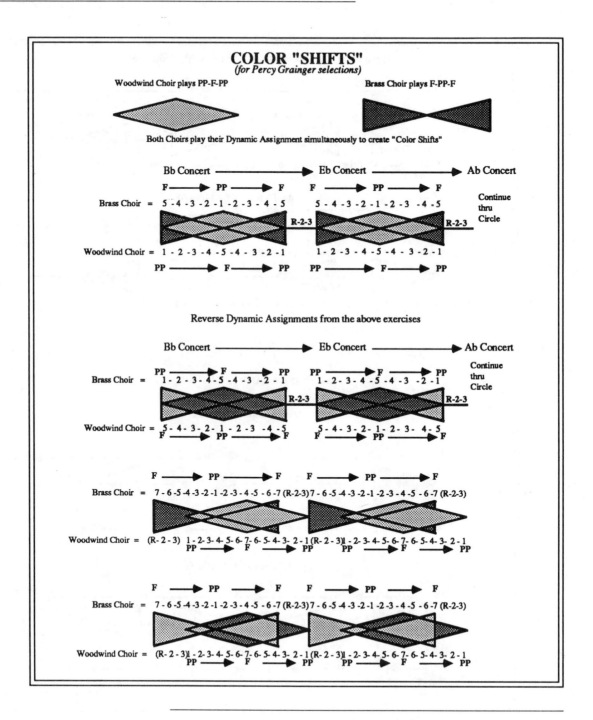

COLOR "SHIFTS"
(for Percy Grainger selections)

Woodwind Choir plays PP-F-PP   Brass Choir plays F-PP-F

Both Choirs play their Dynamic Assignment simultaneously to create "Color Shifts"

Bb Concert ⟶ Eb Concert ⟶ Ab Concert

Brass Choir = 5 - 4 - 3 - 2 - 1 - 2 - 3 - 4 - 5   5 - 4 - 3 - 2 - 1 - 2 - 3 - 4 - 5   R-2-3   Continue thru Circle

Woodwind Choir = 1 - 2 - 3 - 4 - 5 - 4 - 3 - 2 - 1   1 - 2 - 3 - 4 - 5 - 4 - 3 - 2 - 1

Reverse Dynamic Assignments from the above exercises

Bb Concert ⟶ Eb Concert ⟶ Ab Concert

Brass Choir = 1 - 2 - 3 - 4 - 5 - 4 - 3 - 2 - 1   1 - 2 - 3 - 4 - 5 - 4 - 3 - 2 - 1   R-2-3   Continue thru Circle

Woodwind Choir = 5 - 4 - 3 - 2 - 1 - 2 - 3 - 4 - 5   5 - 4 - 3 - 2 - 1 - 2 - 3 - 4 - 5

Brass Choir = 7 - 6 -5 -4 -3 -2 -1 -2 -3 -4 -5 - 6 -7 (R-2-3) 7 - 6 -5 -4 -3 -2 -1 -2 -3 -4 -5 - 6 -7 (R-2-3)

Woodwind Choir = (R- 2 - 3) 1 - 2- 3- 4- 5- 6- 7- 6- 5- 4- 3- 2 -1 (R- 2 - 3) 1 - 2- 3- 4- 5- 6- 7- 6- 5- 4- 3- 2 -1

Brass Choir = 7 - 6 -5 -4 -3 -2 -1 -2 -3 -4 -5 - 6 -7 (R-2-3) 7 - 6 -5 -4 -3 -2 -1 -2 -3 -4 -5 - 6 -7 (R-2-3)

Woodwind Choir = (R- 2 - 3) 1 - 2- 3- 4- 5- 6- 7- 6- 5- 4- 3- 2- 1 (R- 2 - 3) 1 - 2- 3- 4- 5- 6- 7- 6- 5- 4- 3- 2- 1

Sforzando (Sfz) and Forte Piano (fp) Entrances

In an attempt to simplify and develop a more consistent approach to these two troublesome musical demands, I have found by approaching such entrances through "numbers" to be highly successful and more easily understood by the students.

More often than not, these two entrances are not definable in musical performance. They usually end up sounding alike, or with very little difference. The sforzando often has a "stinging" quality, with cracked or missed notes. The same holds true for "FFP" entrances. The problem is due to the students not providing enough duration to the initial entrance or coming off the sound to quickly. This causes poor tone quality with little attention to consistency. This instructional technique simply defines exactness and where the sound should diminish and expand.

This technique is only used with slower tempos. Slow tempo provides the students with a reasonable amount of time to process and listen to the quality and differences of "Sfz" and "Fp" entrances.

This technique should be applied after your organization is aware of the exercises used in Crescendo and decrescendo.

Forte Piano (fp or ffp) Teaching Procedure:

The "numbers" will be used slightly different, but will not create any confusion. When dealing with Forte Piano entrances, "1" will no longer imply "soft" or "PP." It will have the same weight or volume as the higher number which we will crescendo to (1's = 7). The number "2" will be Piano, followed by Crescendo on 3, 4, 5, 6 and 7. The example given below will be processed through 7 counts, with "1" having the same volume as "7." This procedure is to be used for Forte-Piano entrances followed by a crescendo to the release.

Example:

1.....2.....3.....4.....5.....6.....7

F.....P..Cres.........................F
(1 and 7 are equal volume levels)

Forte entrance on "1," when the mind thinks of "2," this will be "piano"....then increase volume as you silently count 3, 4, 5, 6, 7.

This exercise should be expanded to 9's, and 11's.

Play exercise around Circle of 4ths in Unison &Octaves and various Chord Qualities.

Sforzando Teaching Procedure:

When developing the "Sforzando" entrance, we simply sub-divide "1" to become "One And" and bring the dynamic level down to Piano on the "and" of 1. This will give you an effective and consistent "sforzando" entrance.

Example:

1....&....2.....3......4.....5.....6.....7
Sfz...P..Cresc...........................FF

This exercise should be expanded to 9's, and 11's.

Play exercise around Circle of 4ths in Unison &Octaves and various Chord Qualities.

This teaching technique clarifies the differences between the two entrances. *It allows more time to focus attention to entrance accuracy and quality while assuring that everyone diminishes at the exact time to create performance effectiveness and consistency.* This procedure establishes effective reference points similar to the dynamic variations dealing with crescendos and decrescendos.

****

Make copies of the Dynamic Illustrations for each student. Students will refer to these when used in the warm-up process of your rehearsal. Chapter 9 provides all the materials to be duplicated for each student in your ensemble.

Chapter 7

The Conductor

The Conductor as The Listener

"Reactionary" Conducting

Control the "Action"

Casual Rehearsal Ears vs. Critical Performance Ears

Pyramid of Auditory Skills

Very little has been written or said about *not conducting* in rehearsals and becoming a *"Listener."* This role does not imply that we are not to conduct complete compositions or selections. It means to "step away" from the score more often during a rehearsal. This occasional "listener" role triggers a totally different auditory response and reaction ! This chapter describes the many advantages of applying this technique including other significant considerations for the director.

The Conductor as The Listener

Balance in instructional techniques must be developed. This balance is achieved by moving from "conductor" to "listener" without feeling the guilt or negligence of not being alert or "guarding" against the smallest error constantly. It is a means of establishing a balance between the growth process and formula. When we are consistently working with formula structure (eliminating errors), a tendency to stifle the students musical potential is possible. *Formula is based upon "pattern" and individuals must fit into this "pattern" instead of shaping the individuals talent without the restrictions or confinements of a formula.* Being able to have confidence and sureness in our ability to recognize the subtlety of expression provides and allows far greater achievement instead of the many tried and tested recipes.

The amount of time we spend before our organizations activates the *analytical-error detector mode* within us. Such a state can eventually consume our every thought while in front of the group with our natural desires to achieve perfection. Our eyes are "fixed" to the score, reacting to the visual accuracy of signs and symbols while our ears are "fixed" to detect and hear the smallest error or imperfection in what our eyes have directed us in hearing. When we are consumed by this state, "the good" can often be overlooked. Eventually, satisfaction and reward only comes from accuracy of the mechanical or mathematical detail, instead of the musical expression. A tendency to lose sight of the organization's purpose can eventually create a *value* only for numerical or mechanical purposes. Rehearsals and performances structured under such conditions can establish a misguided worth or value to musical expression (although, such a performance will usually receive high numerical grades in a contest).

The program which consistently stresses the mathematical and mechanical aspects of music making can very often end up with *contrived performances*. If rehearsals are structured toward the correction of errors (dealing with all signs and symbols which represent a multitude of details placed together in bits and pieces to form the "whole") it more often than not ends as being a contrived expression. *Contrived performances require the conductor to mechanically and methodically create the same expression each time a piece is performed* (is this an artistic expression?). Contrived performances create severe restrictions and leave little room for individual differences in interpretation. The students are being deprived from this non-verbal language of expression. Feelings are not contrived and emotions change from day to day. Subtle differences from day to day must have the freedom to be expressed. Such subtlety with the freedom of nuance and inflection comes after the "detail"(but must be addressed).

Too often students perception of their director is someone who "beats time" in front of the band. Such an environment is easily developed if all our energy and time is consumed with our eyes and ears fixed in and on the score. *The more you remove yourself from the printed score, the more you can express the music that lies within you.*

The difference between conducting with a score and conducting without, alerts two different listening awareness levels. I refer to these two types as: *"Action"* and *"Reactionary"* conducting. By understanding both techniques allows the conductor to move between the two and improve total ensemble performance.

"Reactionary" Conducting

Conducting and using the score is a "Reactionary" form of conducting. This form is an analytical approach (which is absolutely necessary in the early stages of preparation). However, we too often find the conductor with eyes and ears buried in the score. The reading of a score triggers a Left Hemispheric way of processing information and *creates a listening reaction toward anticipation of detail and error.* Listening "through the score" activates a reaction to individuals, sections, key signatures, rhythmic demands, etc. Again, I must stress this to be an important part of our responsibilities and any neglect to these areas would create an undesirable performance. *The critical concern is in how we balance mechanical demands relative to expressive qualities.*

Quite often our imagination (which is a powerful force) takes over and we "hear" the precision of the printed score and tend *not* to "hear" the actual overall performance of our organization ! Our imagination can easily fool us. This is why we must step back frequently and become a "listener" during rehearsals. It is the only way to return to reality and truly hear the band as it *actually* sounds.

Small errors in performance become "big" and tend to temper our final reaction and appreciation for the students overall performance. How often have you attended a concert and informed the band director on how much you enjoyed the performance..... his response was displeasure followed with a statement such as, *"we had some problems with the technical demands".....* or *"the students just weren't up to a good performance tonight."* We all are guilty of such a statement. Such a reaction may be because the performances in which we have been satisfied (if any), were perceived in a more "wholistic" manner, instead of the *analytical-error detector* type of awareness (the difference between Left and Right Mode processing of information).

Conflict between the two listening levels will be more apparent on stage while conducting if we never got out of an error-detector mode during previous rehearsals. I believe, by creating such an awareness through *Action vs. Reactionary* conducting, we can increase performance levels and receive more satisfaction in achieving superior musicianship. Also, the graphic illustration of the *Director Awareness Scale* (Chapter 1), provides a greater insight to our rehearsal and performance structure and how long we stay at the first three levels before moving to the fourth and fifth levels of artistic expression.

Control the "Action"

Without the score, we can take control of the "Action." We listen to the "whole" performance rather than "bits and pieces" and can sense the flow and motion of the total ensemble sound. Most apparent is that conducting without a score becomes a Right Mode of processing our interpretive skills. By understanding this mode of processing allows us to release our inner feelings and perception of musical expression. It creates an avenue for our uniqueness of interpretation to be projected to the performers and audience.

As conductors we should consider research data by the University Associates of California and the Synectics Institute of Massachusetts regarding communication. It has been found that 8% of a message is communicated through Words, 37% is through the tone, nuance and vocal inflections of these Words, and 55 % of this message is communicated through non-verbal body language. With such data, it is important that we give greater consideration to the body language we use when conducting our organizations if we expect improved performance standards. The largest part of the message is communicated by non-verbal body language. The question is, to what degree are we able to use arms, hands, and facial expressions to more effectively project the composers intent.

Conducting patterns really have very little expressive qualities other than larger or smaller patterns, long or short abrupt movements. Freedom to express our inner reactions tend to make us reserved and inhibited. It is a side of us that we don't like to show and if we do show it, it is done with reservation and caution. We have no problems showing happiness or excitement, but we do have problems with romantic expressive characteristics such as sadness, tenderness, and love. Expressing such emotional characteristics is often lacking in facial and hand movements (body language) in conducting. Releasing this potential (stored in our right mode of processing), releases a spontaneous reaction to the beauty of nuance and inflections. Students will react to our conducting gestures that shape "beautiful" phrases.

To gain freedom for the expressive qualities we all hold within ourselves, take an unfamiliar recording of a major symphony orchestra or band and listen to it a few times. While you are listening, don't consume thoughts to any type of analytical (rhythm, melody, etc.) detail. Focus attention to the flow and ease of phrases, energy, tension and relief, softness, lightness, bold, aggressive or gentle characteristics of the music. Then play it again, this time conduct the recording and try not to use the familiar conducting patterns. Try to flow with the phrases and motion of the music *without any type of conducting form!* By removing the familiar conducting patterns requires us to make "sense" out of the expressive movements of our arms, hands, and facial expression. Don't be surprised at how clumsy you will feel in these early experiments of *"NOnSENSE"* movement. *Through NOnSENSE movement we no longer are concerned with RIGHT and WRONG and more easily take the RISK.* In very short time, a spontaneous reaction to the subtleties of nuance and inflection will be quite apparent. Do this frequently and you will gain a considerable amount of freedom with your arms and hands. Such an exercise demands and develops a closer connection with our "soul" to the sound of music and brings us closer to the actual expression. This technique is similar to *mime*. It is a means of expression through body language.

Gradually start using these motions when conducting your ensemble. Be patient with yourself because the change from someone "beating time" to someone who is shaping and controlling the musical expression doesn't happen immediately. *"SENSE"* will shape the *"NOnSENSE"* movements (have confidence). You will notice a significant *expressive* improvement in the performance of your organization after you have removed your natural inhibitions !

When you can gain freedom in your conducting techniques, and start perceiving and implying the motion and flow of phrases in your conducting, the students will automatically react to the visual nature and style of your conducting patterns. Students become secure in the expressive nature of music and direct their performance to this end. No longer will their perception of a conductor be someone who "beats time" !

The musical responsibilities of students changes from subconscious involvement in "exercise," to a conscious involvement in "expression." A greater sense of satisfaction is readily apparent.

"Casual Rehearsal Ears" vs. "Critical Performance Ears"

An important state of awareness arises approximately one to two weeks before a major performance. During this 1-2 week period of time, our listening becomes far more critical and demanding with our musical expectations of the students relative to the earlier rehearsals 1-2 months before. *It is a "state" in which our goals for superior performance conflict with the results of our rehearsal techniques from the introduction of the literature preparation.* It's becoming aware of *"what we didn't do,"* instead of *"what we did."* Two sets of ears are developed, the "Casual Rehearsal Ears" and the "Critical Performance Ears." Such a condition may be the cause of anxiety and tension before a major performance, rather than the anticipation and excitement of musical expression.

Once we have become aware of these states of listening; it is very easy to adjust in our rehearsal and performance expectations. This is done by simply teaching and expecting performance standards in the early stages of literature preparation and *not expecting something in a performance that was not done in a rehearsal setting.* It is impossible to perform at higher levels than what the students have been prepared for. We may believe this to be possible, but it is only the frame of mind we function in during a performance. The more intense concentration leads us to believe such a condition exists.

The objective in this situation is to become more aware of the performance state of consciousness. This awareness is directed to how students are perceiving the performance and whether it is an analytical or expressive mode of processing. We (and students) are not capable of doing something we never did or experienced before.

If we are not aware of these "Critical Ears" of performance, usually throughout the performance each small error keeps building and multiplying in our memory and eventually, plays havoc with the remainder of the concert. The after-effects are experienced in later rehearsals with greater emphasis placed on student *negligence* instead of the director adjusting rehearsal and teaching techniques to accommodate learning abilities of students. *It is a natural shift in responsibilities.... the students looking to the director for help and the director blaming students for not being able to measure up to standards and expectations.* This continued criticism of students often leads the director in search of a new position where there are "ideal" students who can accept such responsibilities. Unfortunately, this is not the answer. *We cannot escape from ourselves, the students only do what we have taught them. They cannot become any better musicians than what we are as a musician, conductor and teacher.*

Pyramids of Auditory Skill

The most phenomenal abilities and skills are demonstrated by the conductor. The conductor has the ability to discern between indistinguishable error and preciseness with all musical demands of quality, balance, blend, intonation, phrasing, rhythms, technique, and dynamics coupled with the individual and section relative to the total ensemble. The myriad of details and considerations are dealt within a spontaneous manner relative to preconceived ideas and impressions. The talent and instructional skill is equally effective with one individual or to hundreds with the same determination for excellence.

spontaneous manner relative to preconceived ideas and impressions. The talent and instructional skill is equally effective with one individual or to hundreds with the same determination for excellence.

Throughout our educational process we learn about study and practice. The effectiveness of our training comes from how the connections of these elements were made to form the *complete conductor*. Our ability to form these relationships with the multitude of information and experience ultimately dictates the quality of organization we will be able to develop when functioning in a professional setting. All things are relative and must deal with balance. It is the knowledge of when to proceed to the next level.

When working with an ensemble, it is the uniqueness each one of us holds within ourselves which makes the difference in the quality of success. This uniqueness comes from how we originally perceived the information and experiences of our early training. It is judgement and evaluation of quality relative to these past experiences. It comes from confidence, security, and belief in oneself that leads us to search for the ultimate in musical expression.

On the following pages, I have tried to unify all elements of superior ensemble performance through a graphic representation. By developing this wholistic approach, and creating an *aural and visual concept of sound*, allows improved rehearsal and teaching techniques. The visual image of this concept is based upon four *Pyramids* to form a *Tetrahedron*. When all four pyramids are effectively unified, we have what I refer to as the *Superior Ensemble Performance Tetrahedron*.

The base or foundation of this *Tetrahedron* is determined *by the quality of the teaching techniques of the Director*. This foundation will determine whether the organization will ever reach the pinnacle or summit. It is the instructional techniques that allow the students to develop the necessary listening skills to move up the pyramids. *The further we proceed to the point of each triangle, the closer all elements become, with the last being total unification.* This "pinnacle" or "summit" is the finest musical performance and expression possible. *This is what*

Pyramids of Auditory Skills

The first triangle of listening skills is based upon the *Individual, Section,* and *Total Ensemble Sound. It creates and establishes an auditory response between individual, section, and group.*

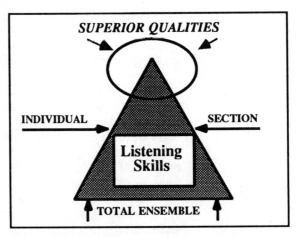

A second triangle of listening skills exists between *Tone Quality, Balance-Blend,* and *Intonation. It creates an auditory response to tone quality relative to the first triangle.*

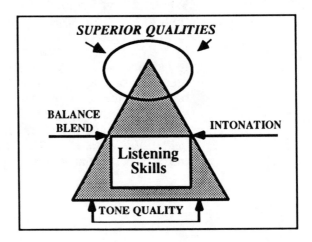

The third triangle of listening skills is based upon *Horizontal* and *Vertical Sound Structure*, and *Chord Color*. *The third triangle creates an auditory and visual response to all elements of sound relative to the entire perceived structure (all three triangles).*

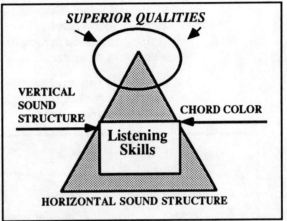

The fourth triangle or base, is the *Conductor. This is the "foundation" in building the Superior Performance Tetrahedron. Its quality is determined by the Conductor's teaching(rehearsal) techniques, musical knowledge-experience, and listening skills.*

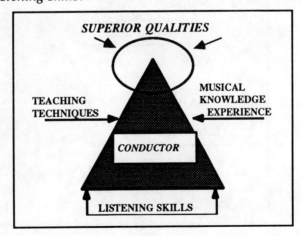

Superior Performance Tetrahedron

The first three triangles form the *PYRAMIDS OF AUDITORY SKILL.* The fourth (conductor) triangle forms the base or foundation to make the *Superior Ensemble Performance Tetrahedron.* These elements determine the organizations level of excellence.

By placing the three pyramids together on the foundation of the conductor (Pyramid #4), we proceed to the peak. This performance quality is determined by the relationships and unification of all instructional techniques and wholistic concepts necessary to integrate all elements of Pyramids #1, #2, and #3.

All are inter-related and based upon the type and quality of rehearsal techniques applied to achieve the desired outcomes in musical performance !

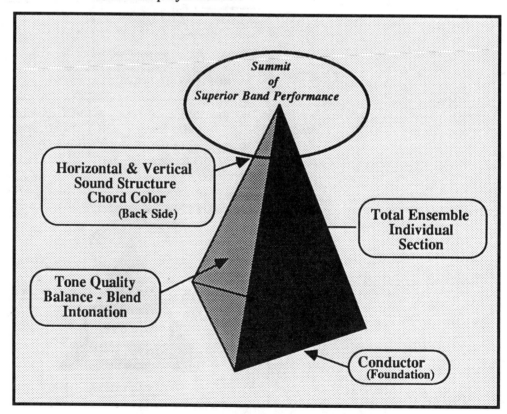

*See page 213 for graphic illustration

Instructional techniques through this concept can be graphically illustrated to form such a wholistic concept thus allowing the director and students greater accessibility to previous linear and sequential techniques which were verbally connected.

The success of this concept is determined by the directors ability to "tailor" the ensembles sound to his inner perception. The directors inner concept of sound *is the difference between superior, average, or poor musical performance.* The capability and potential is there to create and produce the finest imaginable band sound.

This thought process alone will develop the clarity and definition which we strive to develop in our bands. When applying this to literature, you will achieve results that might have taken many years to acquire. This system of musical learning removes many of the mental obstacles and misconceptions held by students. It removes the negative restrictions which so often accompany band performances.

Music is an extremely "humbling" experience.....
a conductor never achieves the expectations of the creator.....
all we can do is make a life long commitment with our practice, study, knowledge, and wisdom, so that our interpretation will be respectful to the creator.....
Once we feel that our musical achievements have reached our expectations....
"mediocrity" will exist.

Chapter 8

Success Techniques

The "secrets" found in this chapter create a unique and positive learning process for students. They are designed to consume all mental energy and not allow room for other thoughts to clutter the students mental and musical process. The examples and exercises contained will aid understanding and resolution of the more frequently abused performance problems.

Our concentration can be sustained when we have clear goals. *Uncertainty makes it easy for our concentration to wander.* Most significantly, the techniques make the mind function more realistically in a music making process... that is "doing one thing..... while thinking of another..... then responding immediately to what was thought of while doing the first thing." Or more aptly stated by Dr. Frank Bencriscutto, Director of Bands at the University of Minnesota: *"At all times are you conscious of what is happening at the moment while relating to what has past, and considering how it will effect what is to come ?"* This is realism in music making. Mentally and physically we are "honing" a technic (like no other) that deals with auditory, visual, and tactile skill simultaneously.

Creating a Mental Shift

In Chapter 1, information was presented regarding hemisphericity and its implications toward effective musical performance. To gain access to our artistic or expressive side, teaching techniques can be created to keep the left brain out of the task or assignment. Split Brain studies indicate the left brain prefers not to give up tasks to the Right, unless it really dislikes the task which may take too much time or is too slow. The left brain is dominant and is always ready to rush in with words and symbols. When the Left Mode is turned off, and the Right is active, a slightly changed state of consciousness is apparent. The objective is to understand when the Left Mode is hampering the students learning process, and to be able to change and shift teaching techniques to achieve the desired result.

126

Visualization and imaging allows us to gain access to this mode shift and experience our "artistic senses." The Right brain takes over and allows the student to shape phrases and to perceive them holistically, allowing the "senses-feelings" to become more apparent. The Right will lead to a "feeling" of closeness, a sense of timelessness, a feeling of confidence, and a difficulty in using words to describe this "feeling."

To achieve this experience and release the students expressive potential from our daily, technical-analytical routine, outlined below is a teaching technique which allows the student and director to experience such a shift into an artistic frame of mind.

Free Improvisation

The one and only way of breaking through this barrier is by *free improvisation.* The term *improvisation* causes many musicians to become tense and insecure. The mere thought of playing without written music and *correct* notes is difficult for many musicians to cope with. A barrier of self consciousness is very evident. When we can break through this negative self judgement, our images of beauty, color, feelings, and emotions become a part of the sounds which we produce.

By introducing students to *free improvisation,* right and wrong notes cease to exist. After a few short practice sessions, the quality of the students performance takes on these musical characteristics when returning to written notation.

The following two examples introduce your students to *free improvisation.* An awareness is immediately apparent between the two modes of processing thought.

The first set of directions will allow the student to only function through the Left Mode of processing. It causes the mind to focus all thinking to the mathematical-mechanical structure. The internal struggle to process the many "details" restricts the students musical ability.

Example #1

Instruct the student to play a *beautiful lullaby* or a melody with the following directions:

> *"Play a slow, beautiful lullaby or ballad. Play it in the key of F major (or any other teacher selected key), using whole, half, quarter, dotted quarters and eighths (or any type of rhythm the teacher assigns). The time signature will be 3/4 time."*

The directions will *clutter* the mind with many "details" which can only be processed in a linear-analytical style. *The result will be a very unmusical performance.*

It will be important to note the students reaction with this first try. They will feel quite uncomfortable with this exercise trying to meet all demands of the directions. Although, not as uncomfortable as the next exercise (#2) because there is some security in the directions which give a base or foundation to start upon.

While they try to play the example, listen for the lack of musical direction, rhythmic problems, and generally, the clumsy melodic flow. The mind is cluttered with "details" and the student is trying to satisfy the directors expectations and directions.

The following directions will only allow the student to function through the Right Mode of processing. *It causes the mind to function in a wholistic sense and focus thinking and listening to the "whole."* They are not thinking of any specific note or musical detail, only starting from a "sound" and creating the melody from that point on.

Exercise #2

After experiencing Step #1, give the following directions:

> *"Play a beautiful lullaby or ballad; start on ANY note, don't be concerned with any specific key, note values or rhythms, and focus your attention on the beauty of the notes you are playing. Don't be concerned with the direction or number of the notes, only your feeling of beauty. Your sense of beauty will lead the notes in a natural direction."*

This type of direction does not address the many details of key, rhythms, etc.. It creates an "image or impression" of the task which is simply a "beautiful lullaby." The left mode cannot function with this type of direction (it's "locked out"), the results must come from the right side where our creative and intuitive senses are located.

Note the student reaction with this exercise. Their first experience with *free improvisation* makes them feel inhibited, self-conscious, and embarrassed. Their reaction is usually, *"I can't do this without the music."* Frequently they'll ask you what note to start on. The first melodies will be quite short with many stops. With caring assurance and positive reinforcement, encourage the student to extend and lengthen the melody each time it is played. As the student continues, you will hear the melodies become more lyrical and start to flow freely. *You will hear a more expressive character and beauty in their playing.* Musical direction and notes will be natural, the student's concentration is totally absorbed in listening to the "beauty" and "feelings" of the melody being created.

Through this form of expressive experience, we become sensitive to the left and right mode interpretations of musical phrases. To hear the differences between Exercise #1 and #2 (and how restrictive #1 is), return to Exercise #1 and give similar directions. You and your student will be quite surprised at the difference.

This *free form* of playing should be a part of daily practice for a few minutes each day. It is the *only* approach which allows the student to "free" themselves of the mathematical-mechanical restrictions of early instruction. This musical experience simply starts with *"nonsense"* and gradually evolves into *"sense."* Unfortunately, the mind spends a significant amount of time directed to mechanics instead of listening. With continued practice, the exercise breaks down these barriers. It brings about a quick awareness of how sterile and uncharacteristic one plays. Gradually, what was perceived as *"nonsense"* notes, now becomes more connected. All listening and attention is directed to lyricism with a natural response to rhythmic sense. The student starts to realize the true meaning of expressive music making. *It is a tremendous method in making a true connection between perception and projection of internal musical expression.*

The next phase of this important instructional technique is to transfer this musical sensitivity into the literature being performed in a large ensemble, solo, quintet, etc.

Teaching Procedure:

1. Direct the student to look at a phrase and silently sing this phrase to themselves. Encourage them to project the "feeling" of expression when they were playing "free form melodies" To alert these "feelings" it may be necessary to have the student play a free improvised melody again and remember how it "feels."

2. *Do not have the student sing aloud.* They become preoccupied with pitch, vocal quality, and intervals. Singing a musical phrase is extremely important but should not be attempted at this stage..... *we are removing restrictions and building confidence !*

3. Allow the student time to internalize the subtleties of nuance and inflections. When the student feels comfortable with what they are silently singing (and holding the feelings of nuance, inflections, and shadings in their "minds eye"), proceed to the actual performance of the written musical phrase.

130

4. Several interpretations should be performed. Have the student choose an interpretation and repeat the phrase which they believed to be most expressive *(it is important that this be the student's choice and not the director's choice)*.

Through this process, your student will be experiencing an *artistic expression* and it will be *theirs !* This initial expressive experience is the beginning of new values for the student. Do not criticize its immaturity, only *encourage*. The students foundation to artistic expression is in place, ready for the director to *shape and develop*.

Your patience and encouragement are critical at this time. Students feel quite inhibited when trying to project their inner feelings. *You should never ask the student to "verbalize" their feelings. This will always stifle any form of creative expression. Such question-answer techniques only trigger the students response to satisfy the directors interpretation and not theirs. The entire process is building confidence in the students expressive and interpretive qualities.* Impatience, both from director and student, will be the only barrier and restriction that you will encounter.

The procedures and experiences presented through *free improvisation* are the only means for the student to experience the subtleties of artistic expression. They first focus attention on the natural feeling and reaction to a lullaby or ballad (every individual has experienced the beauty and sensitivity of the Brahm's Lullaby). From this initial step, we proceed to the many expressive needs of musical interpretation.

The following examples will give you some ideas for the further development of this teaching technique.

Play a free form improvised melody which will:

a. project the "feeling" of a happy, carefree, jolly person skipping down the street.
b. project a solomn, somber, tear-filled, sad person who has just lost his best friend.
c. soar and glide like an eagle in the sky.
d. create a "question" and then play the "answer."
e. project the grace and poise of a ballet dancer on stage.

    f. imagine a big ballroom dance floor in the time of Mozart, the people are all dressed in their finest proper attire.....play an appropriate piece of music for the people to dance to.

    g. imagine the colors of a rainbow....play the sound of blue, red, green, yellow, gold.

    h. project the feeling of *"energy."*

    i. project the feeling of *"intensity."*

    j. project the feeling of *"peace and tranquility."*

This list is unlimited. You can use any type of verbal descriptor to create a situation of *feeling* which can be projected through sound. Not only does this approach *sensitize* the student, but it also stimulates your imagination and enhances teaching concepts no longer directed only to a specific analytical detail.

You will be pleased with the results of this instructional process !

Correcting Technical Irregularities

The brain is made up of billions of neurons. The point at which two nerve cells meet is called the *Synapse*. The synapses determine whether a pulse is transmitted from one cell to another. It is currently thought to be closely involved in the encoding of memory. (P. Russell, 1979). The small space between these cells is thought to be where the chemical and electrical reaction takes place to form memory. These connections for memory are made by *repetition and pattern.* Whenever something needs to be recalled, the activity triggers off this chemical reaction between the cells synapses. *The habit or pattern of that activity when originally learned is then produced (correct or incorrect).*

By understanding this process, we can create a new approach and perspective to "practice." Practicing improperly or practicing material which was not thoroughly presented by the teacher (without complete understanding by the student) will cause many problems. The results are usually a tremendous amount of wasted time and awkward musical performance. When recall of a particular musical pattern is necessary, the recall is riddled with mistakes. *The synaptic connections must be rearranged to establish success connections !*

Teaching Procedure:

1. Student is to analyze the scale fragments found in the technically difficult passage. They can do this if Digital Patterns are a part of the total instructional process (Chapter 2).

2. Re-bar (rhythm) the technically difficult patterns.

3. The student will perform the re-barred group of notes several times. Re-barring should be done with diatonic progressions, easy intervals, etc. to create smoothness and flow of the technical pattern.

4. When you hear the smoothness of the re-barred technical passages, then return to the original barring and rhythmic grouping of notes.

You have established effective learning and practicing procedures for your students if they can analyze technically difficult patterns through digital patterns or sequences, keys and re-barring. This approach creates an entirely different *feeling* for the passage. Eventually, the students will develop this approach in their day to day practice.

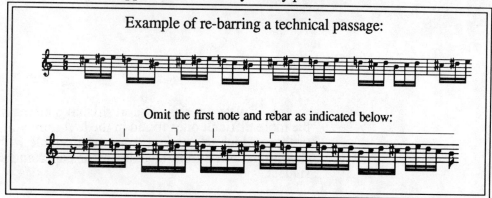

Example of re-barring a technical passage:

Omit the first note and rebar as indicated below:

Imaging Rhythm Patterns

Many instructional techniques and method books have been written in an attempt to teach students to play rhythm patterns at first sight. We strive to achieve a reaction similar to our everyday reading of books, literature, newspapers, magazines, etc. We have even gone to the point of writing and compiling large numbers of rhythm patterns. After many years of applying such techniques, the conditions do not change.... students still have difficulty in reacting to various rhythms.

This approach is unrealistic because it never deals with the most significant need. That is, a spontaneous mental reaction to rhythms when they are needed. This spontaneous reaction is similar to what really happens when we see the simple word *CAT*. In a period of several years, how often is it necessary to practice writing and saying the word *"CAT"* ? But, in music we continue to teach (over several years), basic rhythms such as eighth-quarter-eighth, or dotted eighth-sixteenth, etc.

To achieve and acquire the skill of spontaneous reaction to simple and complex rhythms, calls for instructional techniques that clarify and activate a mental awareness instead of a physical unrelated process.

The teaching technique which is outlined below is a composite of many approaches with the addition of *"imaging."* *It creates a spontaneous response to this image. This technique will work best when working with only one student in a lesson situation.*

Teaching Procedure:

1. Create a series of short rhythm patterns (it's best to use the more difficult ones found in the literature you are preparing or those which the student is not comfortable with). Write this rhythm pattern on the blackboard or paper and show it to the student.

2. Once the student has seen the rhythm pattern, remove it and be sure the student remembers what they saw (the picture).

3. Tap a comfortable pulse or beat in which the student can play the given rhythm pattern.

4. The student will first sustain a long tone (absolutely no measurement of this note such as whole note etc.) *while "imaging" the given rhythm pattern.*

5. Inform the student that while they are sustaining this note and "imaging" the rhythm pattern, you will cut them off. They are to play the rhythm pattern immediately after your cut off.

Always stress to the student that they must be able to "see" the subdivision of the rhythm pattern in their "minds eye" and *play back what they have "seen" rhythmically!*

The initial reaction will leave much to be desired. *And this is exactly what happens in sight reading and other performance situations. You have now discovered the lack of integrated thought processes which is an absolute necessity in superior performance.* The differences are (before such a teaching technique existed), we consumed inordinate amounts of time with repetition and hoping that someday it will work, never really getting to the source of effective learning and application of understanding.

Continue with this teaching technique over an extended time and your results will far surpass any other approach.

The two most significant results will be:

1. Spontaneous reaction to perceived rhythm; the ability to immediately react and perform a rhythm pattern (similar response as to reading "CAT."

2. Create and generate internal motion and direction; the ability to mentally energize a long or sustained note.

Entrance and Sound to Infinity

All techniques and concepts found in this method consistently focus attention to integrated thinking procedures. When synchronized and unified within the *entire* organization, the results are truly remarkable.

Another exceptional performance skill a conductor can experience is to have the enitire organization *enter and release* a sound without any form conducting, rhythm pattern or measurement. Such a skill is possible and creates an intense form of concentration, sensitivity, and mental "energy" within the *entire* band. This sensitization is created through the subtleties of the directors voice and the breathing of the entire organization. The effects upon the entire ensemble establish an acute awareness to the smallest detail while experiencing what it feels like to function as "one."

The subtleties deal with the pulse of the vocal command of *"Exhale and Inhale"* followed by the entrance of sound. The first exposure to this technique is done with the Circle of 4ths and Major Chord grouping assignments. As the concept develops, have students close their eyes. *Within a short time the students will be able to play major chord qualities around the Circle of 4ths WITHOUT vocal command of exhale and inhale. They sense the entire organization as ONE, breath together and make a perfect entrance and release..... you will also become sensitized to your organizations intensity of concentration !*

Exercise #1

Using the Circle of 4ths and Major Chord Quality grouping assignments, give the following directions, slowly:

> *"EXHALE"....pause...."INHALE".....then at the "natural feeling of entrance," allow the entire organization to sound the major chord. Do this between each Major chord around the Circle of 4ths.*

You and your students will be surprised at the accuracy and quality of entrance. There will be some imperfections in the early stages but don't give up on this important process. *It is another "step" into the artistic frame of mind, performance and expression.*

Once you have achieved moderate success (remember, we are building the subtle awareness of artistic expression) with this exercise, proceed to Exercise #2.

Exercise #2.... Sound to Infinity

This process will call for the students to close their eyes while playing. It will be necessary to *Visualize and Image* sound to infinity, or silence. Also (as you read in an earlier chapter), it is *not how a sound is released or stopped*, but *how silence starts !*

Using the Circle of 4ths and unisons and octaves (not major chord qualities), follow the same *"exhale and inhale"* procedures. This time the students will *"diminish the sound to infinity or the beginning of silence !"*

It is important that the concepts of Horizontal and Vertical Sound Structure found in Chapter 3 be referred to in addition to the following:

1. *Create one unified sound, without distinguishing any individual or section* (Horizontal Sound Structure awareness, Balance, Blend, Intonation, Tone Quality).

2. Taper and diminish this sound to *infinity,* being alert to the *"beginning of silence ."* (Horizontal Sound Structure)

3. Upper voices and sections will start *silence* (release) slightly before tenor, baritone and bass voices. Upper voices *blend or "melt" into fundamental (group 4).* Stress Vertical Sound Structure awareness, Balance, Blend, Intonation, Tone Quality.

Don't be discouraged with the early results. Recognize the potential of such a teaching technique. Our normal day to day rehearsal procedures have not alerted the students to think or listen in this manner. It is very demanding and actually exposing the individual and organization to undisciplined mental control. This is a tremendous teaching technique which develops an intense form of concentration and an awareness to total ensemble sound.

Exercise #3

Once you have achieved moderate results with Exercise #2, proceed with the Circle of 4ths, playing Major Chord qualities (and other) through grouping assignments.

It will be important to outline the same three procedures found in Exercise #2 plus those found in Chapter 3 on Horizontal and Vertical Sound Structure. Review concepts and techniques dealing with *Chord Color*. They are important when doing this exercise !

Imaging Perfection

Imagination deals with *entirety and can see the finished product*. This phenomenal resource (which we all are born with), often goes unused or receives little attention. The jazz artist is gifted in this sense. He can "see" his expression through his "minds eye" and without fear, take the "risk" and bring this spontaneous expression to reality.

The mind cannot discern between real or imagined experiences (correctness and incorrectness). When we use our imagination, it is *error free*. We can hear perfection in our "minds eye." It is only the mental understanding, not physical (the students are already aware of embouchure, fingerings, etc.), which is important. If the proper mental understanding and process is in place, the mind will direct the muscles to produce the imagined expectation. If the phrase or passage is properly understood by the students, *they will not hear mistakes!*

We can use this phenomenal resource in our day to day teaching techniques. It can immediately solve technical problems, articulation, uneven rhythmic flow, balance, blend, or other musically related problems. The only obstacle in our way is suspicion. Because it is not part of the daily repetition, we have reservations in applying such teaching techniques.

This teaching technique removes negative reaction, consuming mental energy toward *"I can't play this"* or *"I'll never be able to play this."* This type of response is normal for humans because it assures us that we really can't do it. Psychologists often refer to this as *roof brain chatter.* This is the barrier which consumes more mental energy than the task itself. It reassures the doubt we hold in ourselves. We can change our direction from negative response to positive input.

Such a technique creates "freedom" from mechanical and physical restrictions in performance. It provides a holistic approach to our natural physical, mental, and technical abilities. We can function without restrictions caused by identifying and focusing attention to smaller isolated details.

I have outlined a very simple procedure. *Apply this only in a small group lesson setting and not in full band rehearsal.* It adapts easily in small group classes because it is a more intimate instructional technique.

Teaching Procedure:

1. The student will play the passage in which there are problems. The problems may be articulation, uneven rhythmic flow, technical or other.

2. Next, the student will *silently "image" playing through this same difficult passage as you conduct* (Yes, you will be conducting their "imagined" performance). Do not focus any attention to any of the difficulties experienced earlier. *Do this Imaging at least three times to assure no unnecessary attention to any preconceived problems.*
The director should also silently "image" playing along with the students to create a closer connection and "feel" of the teaching technique.

3. After you have done the above Imagery exercise, have the student play exactly what they heard in their mind ! You will notice a significant improvement and more often than not; *it will be perfect !*

If problems are still evident, return to steps first 2 steps of this process. An apprehensive feeling is still being contained and is restricting the intended performance. Clarify any problems with rhythms or fingerings.

Independent Concentration

Throughout this method and system of musical learning, we have used numbers to activate the mind. By using the number's value, many applications can be made in music making other than just beats in a measure. Numbers were used in the Measurement of Sound and Silence (Chapter 5) to develop synchronized and unified thinking within the entire ensemble. Once you have established such controlled and timed concentration within the entire ensemble, the next logical step in musical development is *creating independent concentration skill.*

This technique simply *fine tunes* the individual students thinking process to the smallest detail and perfection. The introductory level stresses individual reaction to "beats" within a group of students. As this process develops, the independent reaction to the smaller sub-divisions are applied.

Teaching Procedure:

1. With a small group of students (3 to 8), assign each one a number (to the number of students in the class).

2.   Select a scale. Repeat each scale step relative to the number of students in the class. Each student will play the scale tone on their number and rest on the numbers of the other students in the class. Proceed up and down the scale. *Scales are not written, student must remember number played.*

Do this exercise occasionally in a lesson setting. The first experiences with such an assignment will be difficult for the students because they are accustomed to playing in and following a group. *It is an exercise which creates independent control and confidence in the students thinking process.*

When students can respond to all "down beats," continue with more complex demands in sub-divisions (eighth rests and notes, sixteenth rests and notes).

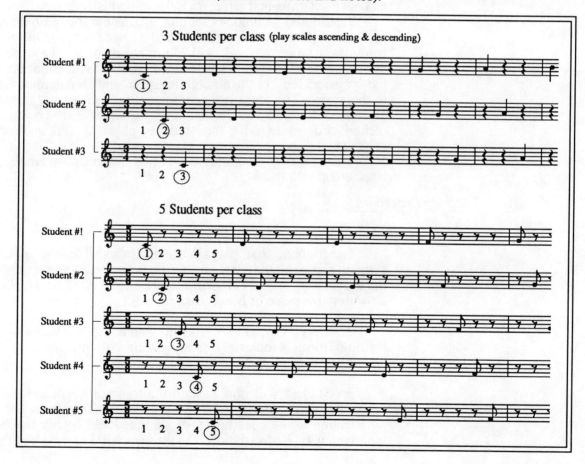

Scale Smoothness and Breath Support

Frequently we hear students play scales uneven because of inconsistent breath support. The air column is not flowing through the instrument with consistent speed. When this occurs, we hear individual notes that "pop" out and have more emphasis than others. Such a performance problem can be attributed to fingering problems within the scale itself (for clarinet players going over the "break"), instrument moving or shaking while playing the scale, and others. This type of condition can create unintended rhythms (uncalled for accents) and have a detrimental effect on Balance and Blend.

Traditional techniques require a considerable amount of time to acquire the smoothness that is necessary. Outlined below is a process which will eliminate many of these poor performance problems. The student first directs all attention to the "physical feel" of the air column speed and then applies this to the scale. The teaching technique simply creates a greater awareness to need and reason for smoothness. It creates a mental connection with the students physical and auditory response.

This teaching technique is equally successful in small or large group settings.

Teaching Procedure:

1. Student first plays scale in straight quarter notes, slurring and sustaining last note as a whole note. Do not repeat the top note of scale. This will require a total of 18 beats. Tap a comfortable pulse or beat (quarter = 60).

2. Point out to the student where the unevenness is coming from: inconsistent speed of air column, tense hand position or fingerings, horn moving, etc.

3. Student will now sustain the tonic or keynote for 18 beats at a *mezzo forte* or *forte* dynamic level. They must focus all attention to the consistency of air speed and breath support without any type of variation. The director will keep track of the

number of beats sustained and cut off after 18 beats. Student is to direct all attention to what this perfectly straight line of sound "physically feels" like, with constant air speed,embouchure, breath support. Visualize a straight line of sound (Horizontal Sound Structure).

4. Do the same thing a second time. *While sustaining and maintaining this "physical feeling," mentally play the scale in your mind.*   The sustained pitch must not have any imperfections while *mentally processing the scale !* Also, the sustained note will come out to be 18 beats if the student mentally plays the scale while sustaining the keynote/tonic.

5. Now, the student will actually play the scale but this time, *mentally sustain the tonic or keynote in their mind* (reverse the thinking procedure), and *RETAIN the "physical feeling" of constant air speed, fixed embouchure, etc. while moving fingers through the scale.* Simply, imagine you are playing the sustained note while picking up or putting down your fingers.

This is a difficult concept. It is a two step mental process. First, attention is directed to sustaining one note while focusing in on air column (speed, physical feel). Second, attention is directed to mentally moving fingers while sustaining this note. The second step is simply a reversal of playing the scale while focusing thinking to the sustained tonic or keynote.

Similar concepts and procedures are applied to the development of phrases. The usual situations, as described above with scales, are evident in student performance of phrases. Continue this process with phrase development as outlined below.

Phrase Development

The instructional procedure used for creating smoothness and intensity of phrases, is directly related to the Dynamic exercises found in the Variations of Chord Qualities and the Measurement of Sound and Silence.

To eliminate phrase problems such as notes "poppng" out (uneven air column speed or breath support) lack of crescendo or decrescendo, unaware of "peaks" or phrase direction, lack of intensity, etc., follow the instructional procedures below.

Teaching Procedure:

1. Add the total number of beats within the phrase and determine the "peak" of the phrase by number (7,8,9,10, et c.). Phrase numbers can vary in length. Example: If a phrase is 17 beats long, and the "peak" is on count number 9, the diminuendo of the phrase will be processed as 8,7,6,5,4,3,2, and the release is 1.

Or if the phrase has two or more peaks then it would be processed as: 1, 2, 3, 4, 5, 4, 3, 2, 1, 2, 3, 4, 5, 6, 7, 8, 9, 8, 7, 6, 5, 4, 3, 2, 1.

2. Put these mathematical combinations together and use the starting pitch of every phrase and sustain only that pitch throughout the number sequence. Increase the volume as the numbers increase, and decrease volume as the numbers decrease.

This is a very simple process but effective. Throughout the students entire educational process, numbers have simple meaning and value which are very easy to respond to. There is no doubt about the numbers correctness or value. All we have done is made a mental connection with volume relative to number value.

3. Stress the physical "feeling" of expanding and contracting the sound of one note relative to the numbers they are processing mentally.

4. Do the same thing again as in #3, but this time mentally process the written notation while sustaining the first note for the duration of the phrase. Stress the need to "physically feel" the air column increase and decrease while *imaging* the flow of the phrase.

5. Lastly, apply this same "physical feeling" and move fingers for the pitches written.

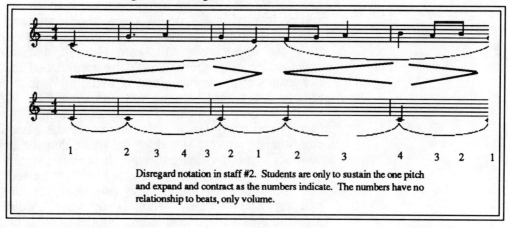

Disregard notation in staff #2. Students are only to sustain the one pitch and expand and contract as the numbers indicate. The numbers have no relationship to beats, only volume.

Developing Musical Motion

Why do some bands play with excitement, energy, beauty, expression and all the characteristics which attract us as listeners while others simply "never get up off the ground"? Simply, being able to have an organization which accurately places all notes and details is not music making. Most important is the ability to create an intensity of involved expression within the total ensemble to the composers intent.

Music must have motion. Without motion, it serves no purpose. This is what attracts and holds the listener to the variations of sound and silence. The old jazz adage, *"eight to the bar"* has significant meaning in creating the energy and excitement of jazz music. If we apply this to band performance, we immediately find where the motion and flow of music comes from. *The term "eight to the bar" only means that the musician is capable of "feeling" the sub-divisions of a measure, section or composition.* Once we can sense and control such a feeling, and are able to "ride the wave" of this musical motion, the music will "live" and no longer be stagnant.

Having students trained in responding to sub-divisions (or "eight to the bar"), allows us greater access to many more musical needs. Playing a march written in 2/4, but rehearsed and performed in 4/8, opens a new door to musical expression, interpretation and accuracy. *Not only access to accuracy, but truly the opportunity to create the life and energy of the composition.* All music should be approached in this manner. For instance: if a composition is written 4/4, then perform it in 8/8, or 2/4 would become 4/8, 6/8 would be 12/16 and 3/8 would become 6/16 etc. The important aspect is to create the motion and energy of *double time* under the basic 2/4, 4/4, 6/8 etc. time signature. This does not mean that the conductor will conduct a sub-divided pattern ! It is only the ability to sense and feel the energy which is created by such a concept.

To apply this concept in rehearsal situations does not call for extraordinary amounts of time. Although, a few prerequisites will be necessary. Students must understand the concepts and techniques outlined in Chapter 5 and understand the doubling of all note values.

Introductory experiences in this concept are best achieved by using a march written in 2/4 or Cut Time. Follow the procedures outlined below.

Teaching Procedure:

1. Play through the march in its entirety. Focus your attention to the ensembles consistent (or inconsistent) pulse or beat. Conduct the pattern designated by the time signature.

2. Before playing the march again, choose a student percussionist who can play consistent eighth notes with precision and evenness on a snare drum. Have the snare drum start playing eighth notes at a *forte* dynamic level so as this will be the most apparent sound when the band starts to play. As the snare drum is playing, alert the students to the motion, flow, and consistency of the eighth notes.

3. While the snare drum is playing the constant eighth note pattern (not the written snare drum part) bring the band in and play through the introduction and first strain. At the end of the first strain, stop the band but still have the snare drum continue to play eighth notes. Again, alert the students to the motion, flow, and consistency of the snare drum (speak over the snare drum playing). Keep the snare drum playing.

4. Play the introduction and first strain a second time. Stop the entire band and snare drum at the end of the first strain. Pause and direct the students to silently imagine the sound of the snare drum and eighth notes. Give them a few seconds to imagine the sound and *feel the motion* of eighth notes.

5. Start the march again, without any snare drum or other percussion. Direct the students to hear and feel the sound and motion of the snare drum as they play through the Introduction and first strain. If you sense any discrepancies with the double time pulse, stop and have the snare drum play eighth notes again.

6. Continue developing the entire march. If the trio section is written *"p"* or *"pp"* most likely the tempo will slow down. The procedures outlined with the snare drum and "imaging" the pulse will immediately break these many "bad habits." *When a band slows down in soft passages, they have been conditioned to watching the director "beat time" and not trained in maintaining an "internal ensemble pulse."*

Continue this process with and without the snare drum. Once you have established this approach, vary it throughout rehearsals. Whenever a situation arises with tempo stability, or creating motion, energy or flow within a selection, quite often, by briefly alerting students to maintaining the Internal Ensemble Pulse will suffice.

Frequently, many conductors will attempt trying to conduct a fast sub-divided pattern. Such conducting will always destroy any type of motion or musical energy which the organization is producing or attempting to produce. If the band has not developed an *internal sense of motion and time,* the conductor who is "beating time" in 4, 6, or 8 is not contributing a thing to the performance.

The director is to use musical discretion relative to the outlined procedures. Such an approach (with snare drum playing eighth notes) is not prudent on certain types of literature.

Review Chapter 5 which deals with Rhythmic Perception and Internal Ensemble Pulse.

Conclusion

The instructional procedures outlined in this chapter will allow you to approach many performance problems with a new direction. They are based upon imagery and sensory reactions. The students relate and respond with positive results. The techniques are not "short cuts," but simply create a new avenue for improved learning and performance.

The sensitivities gradually develop over time and the success is determined by the directors ability to "sense" and "feel" learning taking place. It is as though the teacher existed inside the students mind. It is the ability of the teacher to work from within the student, instead of imposing upon or dictating to the student.

The musical performance expectations, responsibilities and quality are based upon the students sequential thought process to attain the desired musical results through logical conclusions.

Chapter 9

Alternative Rehearsal Techniques Outline
Circle of 4ths (Duplicate for students)
Jazz Ensemble, Orchestra, and Chorus Grouping
Measurement of Sound and Silence
Chord Quality Variations
Chord Voicing
Ruler of Time
Rhythm Exercises
Dynamics
Scale Variations
Digital Patterns
Pyramids of Auditory Skills
Listening -Balance, Blend, Intonation
Listening - Beatless Tuning
Suggestions & Reminders

Implementing Alternative Rehearsal Techniques

This Chapter provides a suggested outline for implementing *Alternative Rehearsal Techniques* along with a compilation of examples presented in the previous chapters. Most examples appear in a graphic illustration instead of the standard musical notation. *The removal of written notation emphasizes auditory response and development. The student is able to focus all concentration on the quality of sound being produced !*

It is important to integrate the many warm-up variations with the literature you are preparing. *This is the critical "link" in creating a productive rehearsal.* The concepts presented are the means in which you establish an effective communication line with your students to the common goal of superior musical performance qualities.

The entire process is not one which can be implemented during the first rehearsal, nor is it a series of "page turning exercises" followed throughout year. The system is endless, depending upon your creativity. The unlimited combinations of exercises and variations often finds students anticipating and looking forward to the next rehearsal.

Review the graphic illustration on page χ at the beginning of this text. This creates a broader perspective and wholistic picture of the entire system of musical learning.

Suggested Guidelines and Procedures

This outline serves as an introductory guide for the implementation of *Alternative Rehearsal Techniques*.   It is not necessary to adhere strictly to the outline. Once the basic concepts are introduced, you will easily adapt your own ideas and no longer need to refer to these guidelines.

Month #1.....Week #1

1. Distribute/describe the use of the Circle of 4ths sheet (page 19 & 160, 161)
   a. Make Zerox copies of Page 161 for all students
   b. Transposition
       C Instruments start Circle on Bb
       Bb Instruments start Circle on C
       Eb Instruments start Circle on G
       F Instruments start Circle on F
       Bass Clef Instruments Start Circle on Bb
   c. Instruct students to read from Left to Right and return to starting pitch.
2. Duration exercises - Unisons/Octaves
   a. Sustain 4, 5, 7, & 9 beats (Page 22 & 163)
       Do not relate with any type of note duration
       Attention (Listening) is focused to tone quality and pulse
   b. Do not use "Silence" at this time
       Emphasis is placed on reading letter symbols
3. Include a few of your standard warm-ups
   a. During introductory phase (1st week) alternate
       with standard warm-ups

Small Group Lessons/Sectionals
Reinforce understanding of *Circle of 4ths* and its use
Clarify any questions with duration exercises, etc.
Emphasize the mental accuracy of duration (mental counting/pulse and release)

$\boxed{\textit{Week \#2}}$

1. Introduce Grouping Assignments (page 23 & 161)
    a. Determined by parts/positions played in Band
    b. Group 1, 2, 3, 4
        (alter grouping assignments to serve your instrumentation)
2. Major Chords with Duration of 5, 7, & 9 beats (page 24 & 168)
    Group 4 starts on Root (Bb)
    Group 3 starts on 5th (F)
    Group 2 starts on 3rd (D)
    Group 1 starts on Root (Bb)
3. Include some of the Duration exercises from 1st week
    a. Unisons/octaves
    b. 5, 7, & 9 beats

Small Group Lessons/Sectionals
Introduce and start teaching Beatless Tuning concepts (page 64 & 214)
Logical Conclusions to Effective Intonation (Page 66 & 213)

$\boxed{\textit{Week \#3}}$

1. Measurement of Sound & Silence (page 78)
    a. Describe (Chapter 5)
        The first steps to Unify/synchronize mental timing
        Accuracy and precision will be no better than:
            quality of thinking process = discipline of duration !
        Accuracy/precision is not physical but MENTAL !
2. Exercises (pages 164 & 165)
    Sound 5, silence 3 in unisons
    Sound 7, silence 5 in unisons
    Sound 5, silence 7 in unisons
    Sound 5, silence 3 in major chord grouping (page 169)
    Sound 7, silence 5 in major chord grouping
    Sound 5, silence 7 in major chord grouping
3. Introduce Horizontal and Vertical Sound Structure (page 54 - 56)
    Review Chapter 3...Creating an Aural & Visual Image
4. Introduce Internal Ensemble Pulse with entrance-release
    a. Visualize the accuracy of Entrance on a Vertical basis
    b. Visualize the accuracy of Release on a Vertical basis
    c. Visualize the quality and accuracy of duration-Horizontal
    d. Visualize the Color of this sound on a Horizontal basis

5. Introduce Beatless Tuning Concepts with full band/Tuning from Tuba
       (graphic illustration page 72)
   a. Logical Conclusions to Effective Intonation (Page 66& 213)

Small Group Lessons/Sectionals

Continue Beatless Tuning (Chapter 4)
   Unisons
   Introduce Octave Tuning
   3 Logical steps to Balance and Blend (Page 213) Students recite in order.

Week #4

1. Review Week #3
   a. Major Chords with Sound and Silence
   b. Emphasize accuracy comes from Mental, not Physical process
   c. Emphasize the unification of mental pulse = Internal Ensemble Pulse
      (the location for clarity and definition)
   d. Horizontal and Vertical Sound Structure
   e. Create a Visual Image of these sounds
2. Basic Rhythm patterns with Measurement of Sound-Silence
   a. Use Major chord grouping
   b. Use rhythm patterns from band literature
3. Beatless Tuning with entire band
   a. Logical Conclusions to Effective Intonation (Page 66 & 213)
   b. Follow Tuning procedures on page 72 (graphic illustration)

Small Group Lessons/Sectionals

Continue Beatless Tuning (Chapter 4)
Octave Tuning
Introduce the Tuning of the 5th (page 69)
Review Logical steps to Intonation, Balance and Blend
Introduce Scales around the Circle of 4ths (page 28, 198, & 199)

Month #2....Week #1

1. Introduce Full Ensemble Scale Performance (page 28-32, 199)
   a. Basic Rhythms = Half and quarter notes
   b. Last note of each scale =Think of Next Key/Scale !
2. Measurement of Sound and Silence Exercises Continue
   a. Slowly increase the silence time to 7 to 11 beats (page 83)
   b. Introduce Minor Chord Quality (page 170)
   c. 3 Logical steps to Balance and Blend (page 70)
3. Tune Band from the Tuba - Principal Players (page 72)
   a. Logical Conclusions to Effective Intonation (page 66 & 214)
   b. 3 Logical steps to Balance and Blend (page 70 & 213)

Small Group Lessons/Sectionals

Continue Intonation and Tuning of the 5th (page 69)
Scales around *Circle of 4ths*. Scale Teaching Procedure (page 29-31 & 198)
Introduce *Pyramids of Auditory Skills* & Concepts (page 120-123, 215)

Week #2

1. Introduce Dynamics (Chapter 6)
   a. Decrescendo in Unison/octaves (page 98 & 189)
   b. Decrescendo with Major Chords
   c. Crescendo with Unison/Octaves and Major Chords
2. Review Balance and Blend of Total Ensemble (page 62, 63)
   a. Reinforce 3 Logical steps to Effective Balance and Blend
      Apply these concepts with Dynamic exercises
3. Continue Scale Performance
   a. Half and Quarter Notes
   b. Brass Choir start Scales on Bb Concert
         Woodwind Choir start Scales on F Concert
   c. Scale Variations (pages 32 -36 & 199-204)
4. Tune Band from the Tuba - Principal Players (page 72)
   a. Logical Conclusions to Effective Intonation
   b. 3 Logical steps to Balance and Blend

Small Group Lessons/Sectionals

Review Scale Performance & Scale Variations (pages 32 -36)
Review Scale Teaching Procedure (page 29-31 & 198)
Continue *Pyramids of Auditory Skills* & Concepts (page 120-123, 215)

Week #3

1. Dynamic Exercises (Chapter 6)
    a. Major Chords with sound and silence variations page 191)
    b. Major Chords alternating Choirs (page192)
    c. Review Balance and Blend of Total Ensemble
       Reinforce 3 Logical steps to Effective Balance and Blend
2. Measurement of Sound and Silence Exercises
    a. Introduce Dominant 7th and Major 7th Chord Qualities (Page 172 & 174)
    b. Sound and Silence variations (page 83)
    c. Use rhythm patterns from band literature
    d. Emphasize the unification of mental pulse = Internal Ensemble Pulse
3. Chromatic Scales around Circle of 4ths
    a. Eighth notes slowly in one octave
4. Tune Band from the Tuba - Principal Players (page 72)
    a. Logical Conclusions to Effective Intonation (Page 66 214)
    b. 3 Logical steps to Balance and Blend (Page 70 & 213)

Small Group Lessons/Sectionals
Continue Pyramids of Auditory Skills & Concepts (page 120-123
Octave and 5th tuning procedures (page 67-71)

Week #4

1. Major scales or Chromatic scales with various articulation patterns
    a. Articulation patterns used in band literature
    b. Scale Variations (pages 32 -36)
2. Dynamic Exercises
    a. Using Major 7th or Dominant 7th Chord Qualities
    b. Apply 3 steps to Effective Balance and Blend with 7th tone chords.
3. Measurement of Sound and Silence Exercises (with 7th tone chords)
    a. Sound and Silence variations (page 83)
    b. Use rhythm patterns from band literature
    c. Emphasize the unification of mental pulse = Internal Ensemble Pulse
4. Tune Band from the Tuba - Principal Players (page 72)
    Remind and review Logical Conclusions to Effective Intonation
    Remind and review 3 Logical steps to Balance and Blend

Small Group Lessons/Sectionals
Octave and 5th tuning procedures (page 67-71)
Scales with various articulations (page 199-204)

155

$$\boxed{\textit{Month \#3....Week \#1}}$$

1. Major scales or Chromatic scales with various articulation patterns
    a. Ascend Only
    b. Scale Variations (pages 199-204)
2. Measurement of Sound and Silence Exercises Continue
    a. Sound and Silence variations (page 83)
    b. 3 Logical steps to Balance and Blend (Page 213)
    c. Use chord voicings from band literature
    d. Stress Horizontal and Vertical Sound Structure
    e. Stress the unification of mental pulse = Internal Ensemble Pulse
3. Tune Band from the Tuba - Principal Players (page 72)
    a. Logical Conclusions to Effective Intonation (page 214)
    b. Beatless tuning concepts (Pyramids of Auditory Skills)

Small Group Lessons/Sectionals
Continue to reinforce and expand tuning and listening concepts
Apply instructional techniques found in Chapter 8

$$\boxed{\textit{Week \#2}}$$

1. Basic Digital Patterns and Major scales
    a. Digital (exercises #1 & #2 - page 37 - 43, 206)
    b. Scale Variations (pages 199-204)
2. Rhythm patterns with Measurement of Sound-Silence
    a. Use Major or other chord groupings
    b. Use rhythm patterns from band literature
3. Tune Band from the Tuba - Principal Players (page 72)
    Logical Conclusions to Effective Intonation (page 66)

Small Group Lessons/Sectionals
Continue to reinforce and expand tuning and listening concepts
Apply instructional techniques found in Chapter 8

$$\boxed{\textit{Week \#3}}$$

1. Scale Performance
    a. Ascend the first scale and Descend the next scale (page 202-204)
    b. Scale Variations (pages199-204)

2. Dynamic Exercises
    a. Chord Qualities (7ths, minors, major, etc)
    b. Dynamic variations from literature
    c. Reinforce 3 Logical steps to Effective Balance and Blend
3. Measurement of Sound and Silence Exercises
    a. Sound and Silence variations (page 83)
    b. Use rhythm patterns from band literature
    c. Unify mental pulse = Internal Ensemble Pulse
4. Tune Band from the Tuba - Principal Players (page 72)
    Logical Conclusions to Effective Intonation (page 66)
    Horizontal and Vertical Sound Structure, Color

Small Group Lessons/Sectionals
Continue to reinforce and expand tuning and listening concepts
Apply instructional techniques found in Chapter 8

(Week #4)

1. Scale Performance
    a. Descend the first scale and Ascend the next scale
    b. Scale Variations (pages 199-204)
2. Digital Patterns - relate to scale steps
    a. Digital exercises (page 37 - 43, 206-207)
3. Measurement of Sound and Silence Rhythm patterns
    a. Chord Quality Grouping Assignments (Major, Minor, 7th, etc)
    b. Alternate Brass & Woodwind choir
4. Tune Band from the Tuba - Principal Players (page 72)
    Logical Conclusions to Effective Intonation (page 66)
    Horizontal and Vertical Sound Structure, Color
    Reinforce 3 Logical steps to Effective Balance and Blend

Small Group Lessons/Sectionals
Continue to reinforce and expand tuning and listening concepts
Apply instructional techniques found in Chapter 8

Month #4....Week #1 (Experiment with your own variations)

Scale Performance, vary articulation patterns
    Woodwinds start Scales on F Concert Ascending only
    Brass start Scales on Bb Concert Ascending only
    Scale Variations (pages 199-204)
Measurement of Sound and Silence Rhythm patterns
    Chord Quality Grouping Assignments (Major, Minor, 7th, etc)
    Use Chord voicings from literature
Tune Band from the Tuba - Principal Players (page 72)
    Logical Conclusions to Effective Intonation (page 214)
    Balance, blend, intonation (page 213)
    Horizontal and Vertical Sound Structure, Color

Week #2

Scale Performance, vary articulation
    Chromatic Scales
    Major scales for speed and clarity
        Brass start of Bb Concert
        Woodwinds start on F Concert
Digital Patterns (page 37 - 43, 206-209)
    5 note scales
Measurement of Sound and Silence
    Chord Quality Grouping Assignments (Major, Minor, 7th, etc)
    Rhythm patterns from literature
Dynamic Exercises
    Chord Qualities with silence
    Use Chord voicings from literature
Tune Band from the Tuba - Principal Players (page 72)
    Logical Conclusions to Effective Intonation
    Balance, blend, intonation
    Horizontal and Vertical Sound Structure, Color

Week #3

Scale Performance with Major chord grouping
    Group 1 start scales on Bb Concert
    Group 2 start scales on D Concert
    Group 3 start scales on F Concert
    Group 4 start scales on Bb Concert
    Scale Variations are found on pages 32 -36
Chord Quality Grouping Assignments (Major, Minor, 7th, etc) or
    voicings from literature
    Rhythm patterns from literature
Tune Band from the Tuba - Principal Players (page 72)
    Logical Conclusions to Effective Intonation
    Balance, blend, intonation
    Horizontal and Vertical Sound Structure, Color

Week #4

Scale Performance & Digital Patterns
    Compressing Key Tonality (page 37)
    Digital Patterns
Chord Quality Grouping Assignments (Major, Minor, 7th, etc)
    Apply chord voicings from literature (tutti sections)
Tune Band from the Tuba - Principal Players (page 72)
    Logical Conclusions to Effective Intonation
    Balance, blend, intonation
    Horizontal and Vertical Sound Structure, Color

****

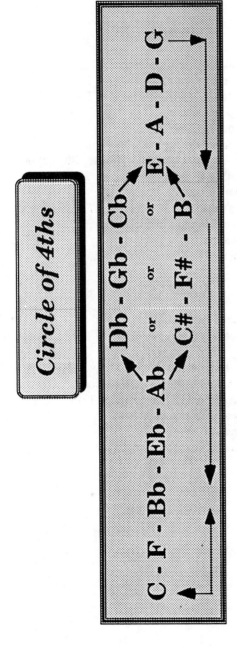

Circle of 4ths

C - F - Bb - Eb - Ab   or   Db - Gb - Cb   or   E - A - D - G

C# - F# - B

INTRODUCTION TO THE CIRCLE OF 4THS SHEET

1. Duplicate and distribute Circle of 4ths sheet to each band member.

2. Instruct students to read from left to right, proceeding through entire circle and returning to their assigned starting pitch.

3. Do not use or refer to any type of written musical notation.

4. Start Circle on Bb Concert: C Instruments start Circle on Bb; Bb Instruments start Circle on C; Eb Instruments start Circle on G; F Instruments start Circle on F.

5. The student has the choice of playing Db, Gb, Cb, or C#, F#, or B (easiest for student).

6. Students are to play pitch in a comfortable range (no extreme high's or low's).

7. First few rehearsals will only address duration exercises for 4, 5, 7, and 9 beats.

The students first reaction will be quite different from the normal rehearsal "habits" established. The removal of musical notation allows the student to focus greater attention to listening. Students develop confidence in what they are "hearing" and focus all attention to the quality of sound they are making ! !

The instructional priority is to activate, sustain, and control students thinking process to the expected musical quality.

Grouping Assignments

Flats →

C – F – Bb – Eb – Ab   or   Db – Gb – Cb (Fb)

1   2   3   4   5   6   7

(B#) (E#) (D#)   (G#)

7   6   5   4   3   2   1

C# – F# – B   or   E – A – D – G

Sharps →

Woodwind Choir

Group 1
Piccolo
Eb Clarinet
Oboe
1st Flute
1st Clarinet
1st Alto Sax

Group 2
2nd Flute
2nd Clarinet
2nd Alto Sax

Group 3
3rd Clarinet
Alto Clarinet
Tenor Sax

Group 4
Bass Clarinet
Bassoons
Bari Sax
Contra Clarinets

Brass Choir

Group 1
1st Cornet
1st Trumpet
1st French Horn
1st Trombone

Group 2
2nd Cornet
2nd French Horn

Group 3
3rd Cornet
2nd Trumpet
2nd & 3rd Trombone
3rd & 4th French Horn

Group 4
Baritone, Euphonium
Tuba
String Bass

Percussion

Group 1
Vibraphone (soft mallets)

Group 2
Xylophone (soft mallets)

Group 3
Marimba (soft mallets)

Group 4
Tympani

(Enlarge and duplicate for students)

Suggested Grouping Assignments for Jazz Ensemble, Orchestra, and Chorus

Alternative Rehearsal Techniques are fully compatible with any type of musical organization. Listed below are suggested grouping assignments for these organizations. Applying these concepts and techniques provides music program continuity.

It will be necessary for you to change and alter the assignments listed to adequately meet your program needs. Jazz Ensemble groupings will require adjustments. I suggest 5 groupings to allow for jazz chord extensions and alterations.

Jazz Ensemble Groupings

Group 1 (octave or 7th)	Group 2 (3rd)	Group 3 (5th)	Group 4 (Root)
1st Alto Sax	2nd Alto Sax	2nd Tenor Sax	Bari Sax
1st Tenor Sax	2nd Trumpet	3rd Trumpet	4th Trumpet
1st Trumpet	2nd Trombone	3rd Trombone	Bass Trombone
1st Trombone	(1st Tenor Sax)	(2nd Trombone)	String Bass

** The above are only suggested groupings. Alter or vary according to harmonic voicing needed.

Orchestra Groupings

** Retain the wind instrument groupings used for band and add the following String assignments.

Group 1	Group 2	Group 3	Group 4
Violin 1	Violin 2	Viola	String Bass
(Violin 2)	(Viola)	Cello	

Instruments appearing in ( ) can be changed to better accomodate organization and director needs.

Chorus Groupings

Group 1	Group 2	Group 3	Group 4
Soprano	Alto	Tenor/Baritone	Bass
	(Soprano 2)	(Alto)	(Tenor/Baritone)

Introductory Duration Exercises

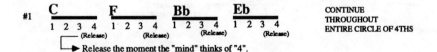

#1 C   F   Bb   Eb   CONTINUE
    1 2 3 4 1 2 3 4 1 2 3 4 1 2 3 4 THROUGHOUT
    (Release) (Release) (Release) (Release) ENTIRE CIRCLE OF 4THS
    ➤ Release the moment the "mind" thinks of "4".

#2 C   F   Bb   Eb   Etc.
    1 2 3 4 5 1 2 3 4 5 1 2 3 4 5 1 2 3 4 5
    (Release) (Release) (Release) (Release)
    ➤ Release the moment the "mind" thinks of "5".

#3 C   F   Bb   Eb   Etc.
    1 2 3 4 5 6 7 1 2 3 4 5 6 7 1 2 3 4 5 6 7
    (Release) (Release) (Release)

#4 C   F   Bb   Eb   Etc.
    1 2 3 4 5 6 7 8 9 1 2 3 4 5 6 7 8 9 1 2 3 4 5 6 7 8 9
    (Release) (Release) (Release)

#5 C   F   Bb
    1 2 3 4 5 6 7 8 9 10 11 1 2 3 4 5 6 7 8 9 10 11 1 2 3 4 5 6 7 8 9 10 11
    (Release) (Release) (Release)

#6 C   F   Bb   Etc.
    1 2 3 4 5 6 7 8 9 10 11 12 13 1 2 3 4 5 6 7 8 9 10 11 12 13
    (Release) (Release)

IMPORTANT

The exactness of the mind processing the numbers ("discipline of duration") determines the quality of entrance, duration and release ! The instructional priority is to unify and synchronize this silent pulse. The quality of the exercise is determined by what occurs mentally from the instant the sound starts (entrance); to what occurs while the sound is being sustained (duration); to effectively contribute to the release !

Measurement of Sound and Silence

Duration Exercises with 3 beats of "Silence" (Refer to Chapter 5)

#1 C   F   Bb   Eb   CONTINUE
   1 2 3 4 Rest 2 3   1 2 3 4 Rest 2 3 1 2 3 4 Rest 2 3 1 2 3 4   THROUGHOUT
        (R)   (R)   (R)   ENTIRE CIRCLE OF 4THS

→ Silently say "Rest 2 3"

#2 C   F   Bb   Eb   Ab Etc.
   1 2 3 4 5 Rest 2 3 1 2 3 4 5 Rest 2 3 1 2 3 4 5 Rest 2 3 1 2 3 4 5 Rest 2 3
        (R)   (R)   (R)   (R)

#3 C   F   Bb   Eb Etc.
   1 2 3 4 5 6 7 Rest 2 3 1 2 3 4 5 6 7 Rest 2 3 1 2 3 4 5 6 7 Rest 2 3 1 2 3 4 5 6 7

#4 C   F   Bb   Eb Etc.
   1 2 3 4 5 6 7 8 9 Rest 2 3 1 2 3 4 5 6 7 8 9 Rest 2 3 1 2 3 4 5 6 7 8 9 Rest 2 3
              (R)   (R)   (R)

#5 C   F   Bb   Etc.
   1 2 3 4 5 6 7 8 9 10 11 Rest 2 3 1 2 3 4 5 6 7 8 9 10 11 Rest 2 3 1 2 3 4 5 6 7 8 9 10 11 Rest 2 3
              (R)   (R)

#6 C   F   Bb Etc.
   1 2 3 4 5 6 7 8 9 10 11 12 13 Rest 2 3 1 2 3 4 5 6 7 8 9 10 11 12 13 Rest 2 3
                      (R)   (R)

5 Beats of "Silence"

#7 C   F   Bb   Eb   CONTINUE
   1 2 3 4 Rest 2 3 4 5 1 2 3 4 Rest 2 3 4 5 1 2 3 4 Rest 2 3 4 5 1 2 3 4   THROUGHOUT
        (R)   (R)   (R)   (R)   ENTIRE CIRCLE OF 4THS

→ Silently say "Rest 2 3 4 5"

#8 C   F   Bb   Eb   Ab Etc.
   1 2 3 4 5 Rest 2 3 4 5 1 2 3 4 Rest 2 3 4 5 1 2 3 4 5 Rest 2 3 4 5 1 2 3 4 5 Rest 2 3 4 5
        (R)   (R)   (R)

#9 C   F   Bb   Eb Etc.
   1 2 3 4 5 6 7 Rest 2 3 4 5 1 2 3 4 5 6 7 Rest 2 3 4 5 1 2 3 4 5 6 7 Rest 2 3 4 5 1 2 3 4 5 6 7
              (R)   (R)   (R)

#10 C   F   Bb   Eb Etc.
    1 2 3 4 5 6 7 8 9 Rest 2 3 4 5 1 2 3 4 5 6 7 8 9 Rest 2 3 4 5 1 2 3 4 5 6 7 8 9 Rest 2 3 4 5
               (R)   (R)   (R)

#11 C   F   Bb   Etc.
    1 2 3 4 5 6 7 8 9 10 11 Rest 2 3 4 5 1 2 3 4 5 6 7 8 9 10 11 Rest 2 3 4 5 1 2 3 4 5 6 7 8 9 10 11 Rest 2 3 4 5
               (R)   (R)   (R)

#12 C   F   Bb Etc.
    1 2 3 4 5 6 7 8 9 10 11 12 13 Rest 2 3 4 5 1 2 3 4 5 6 7 8 9 10 11 12 13 Rest 2 3 4 5
                       (R)   (R)

Sound and Silence Exercises (cont.)

7 Beats of "Silence"

#13   **C**   **F**   **Bb**   Etc.
1 2 3 4   Rest 2 3 4 5 6 7   1 2 3 4   Rest 2 3 4 5 6 7   1 2 3 4
(R)   (R)   (R)

CONTINUE
THROUGHOUT
ENTIRE CIRCLE OF 4THS

→ Silently say "Rest 2 3 4 5 6 7"

#14   **C**   **F**   **Bb**   Etc.
1 2 3 4 5   Rest 2 3 4 5 6 7   1 2 3 4 5   Rest 2 3 4 5 6 7   1 2 3 4 5
(R)   (R)

#15   **C**   **F**   **Bb**   Etc.
1 2 3 4 5 6 7   Rest 2 3 4 5 6 7   1 2 3 4 5 6 7   Rest 2 3 4 5 6 7   1 2 3 4 5 6 7
(R)   (R)   (R)

#16   **C**   **F**   **Bb**   Etc.
1 2 3 4 5 6 7 8 9   Rest 2 3 4 5 6 7   1 2 3 4 5 6 7 8 9   Rest 2 3 4 5 6 7   1 2 3 4 5 6 7 8 9
(R)   (R)   (R)

#17   **C**   **F**   **Bb**   Etc.
1 2 3 4 5 6 7 8 9 10 11   Rest 2 3 4 5 6 7   1 2 3 4 5 6 7 8 9 10 11   Rest 2 3 4 5 6 7
(R)   (R)

#18   **C**   **F**   **Bb**   Etc
1 2 3 4 5 6 7 8 9 10 11 12 13   Rest 2 3 4 5 6 7   1 2 3 4 5 6 7 8 9 10 11 12 13   Rest 2 3 4 5 6 7
(R)   (R)

9 Beats of "Silence"

#19   **C**   **F**   **Bb**   Etc.
1 2 3   Rest 2 3 4 5 6 7 8 9   1 2 3   Rest 2 3 4 5 6 7 8 9   1 2 3 4
(R)   (R)   (R)

CONTINUE
THROUGHOUT
ENTIRE CIRCLE OF 4THS

→ Silently say "Rest 2 3 4 5 6 7 8 9"

#20   **C**   **F**   **Bb**   Etc.
1 2 3 4 5   Rest 2 3 4 5 6 7 8 9   1 2 3 4 5   Rest 2 3 4 5 6 7 8 9   1 2 3 4 5
(R)   (R)   (R)

#21   **C**   **F**   **Bb**   Etc.
1 2 3 4 5 6 7   Rest 2 3 4 5 6 7 8 9   1 2 3 4 5 6 7   Rest 2 3 4 5 6 7 8 9   1 2 3 4 5 6 7
(R)   (R)

#22   **C**   **F**   **Bb**   Etc.
1 2 3 4 5 6 7 8 9   Rest 2 3 4 5 6 7 8 9   1 2 3 4 5 6 7 8 9   Rest 2 3 4 5 6 7 8 9   1 2 3 4 5 6 7 8 9
(R)   (R)   (R)

#23   **C**   **F**   **Bb**   Etc.
1 2 3 4 5 6 7 8 9 10 11   Rest 2 3 4 5 6 7 8 9   1 2 3 4 5 6 7 8 9 10 11   Rest 2 3 4 5 6 7 8 9
(R)   (R)

#24   **C**   **F**   **Bb**   Etc
1 2 3 4 5 6 7 8 9 10 11 12 13   Rest 2 3 4 5 6 7 8 9   1 2 3 4 5 6 7 8 9 10 11 12 13   Rest 2 3 4 5 6 7 8 9
(R)   (R)

Playing Circle in "5ths"
Group Assignments

1.

Groups 1 & 2	F	Bb	Eb	Ab	Db/C#	Gb/F#	Continue thru entire Circle
	1 thru 5	1 thru 5	1 thru 5	1 thru 5	1 thru 5	1 thru 5	Release on "5"
Groups 3 & 4	Bb	Eb	Ab	Db/C#	Gb/F#	Cb/B	
	1 thru 5	1 thru 5	1 thru 5	1 thru 5	1 thru 5		

2.

Groups 1 & 2	F	Bb	Eb	Ab	Continue thru entire Circle
	1 thru 7	1 thru 7	1 thru 7	1 thru 7	Release on "7"
Groups 3 & 4	Bb	Eb	Ab	Db/C#	
	1 thru 7	1 thru 7	1 thru 7	1 thru 7	

3.

Groups 1 & 2	F	Bb	Eb	Continue thru entire Circle
	1 thru 9	1 thru 9	1 thru 9	Release on "9"
Groups 3 & 4	Bb	Eb	Ab	
	1 thru 9	1 thru 9	1 thru 9	

4.

Groups 1 & 2	F	Bb	Eb	Continue thru entire Circle
	1 thru 11	1 thru 11	1 thru 11	Release on "11"
Groups 3 & 4	Bb	Eb	Ab	
	1 thru 11	1 thru 11	1 thru 11	

Choir Assignments

5.

Woodwind Choir	F	Bb	Eb	Ab	Db/C#	Gb/F#	Continue thru entire Circle
	1 thru 5	1 thru 5	1 thru 5	1 thru 5	1 thru 5	1 thru 5	Release on "5"
Brass Choir	Bb	Eb	Ab	Db/C#	Gb/F#	Cb/B	
	1 thru 5	1 thru 5	1 thru 5	1 thru 5	1 thru 5	1 thru 5	

6.

Woodwind Choir	F	Bb	Eb	Ab	Continue thru entire Circle
	1 thru 7	1 thru 7	1 thru 7	1 thru 7	Release on "7"
Brass Choir	Bb	Eb	Ab	Db/C#	
	1 thru 7	1 thru 7	1 thru 7	1 thru 7	

7.

Woodwind Choir	F	Bb	Eb	Continue thru entire Circle
	1 thru 9	1 thru 9	1 thru 9	Release on "9"
Brass Choir	Bb	Eb	Ab	
	1 thru 9	1 thru 9	1 thru 9	

8.

Woodwind Choir	F	Bb	Eb	Continue thru entire Circle
	1 thru 11	1 thru 11	1 thru 11	Release on "11"
Brass Choir	Bb	Eb	Ab	
	1 thru 11	1 thru 11	1 thru 11	

166

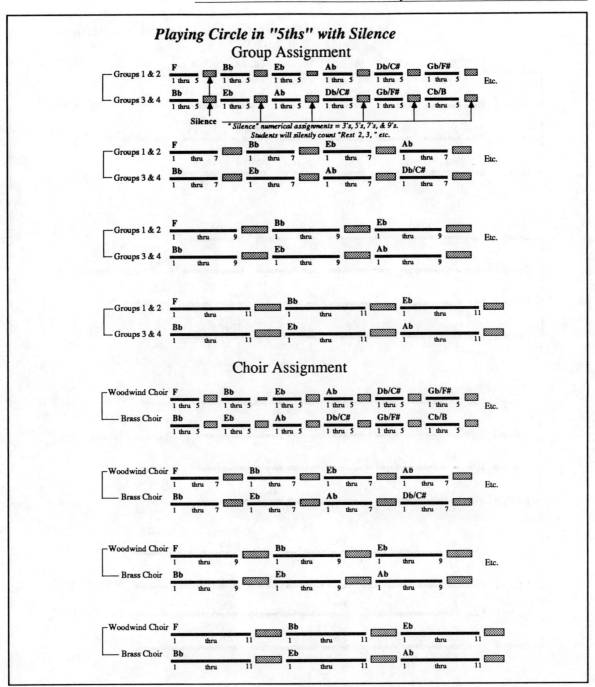

Playing Circle in "5ths" with Silence
Group Assignment

Choir Assignment

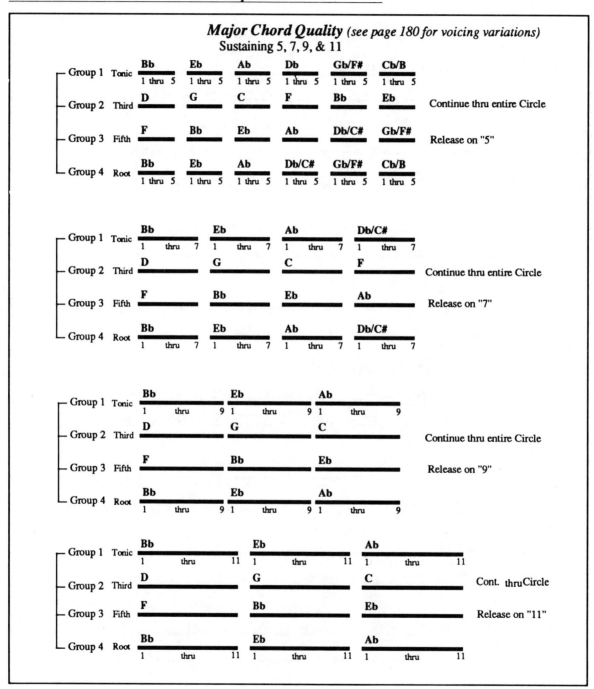

Major Chord Quality (see page 180 for voicing variations)
Sustaining 5, 7, 9, & 11

Major Chord Qualities with Silence
Silence numerical assignments will be 3's, 5's, 7's, & 9's.

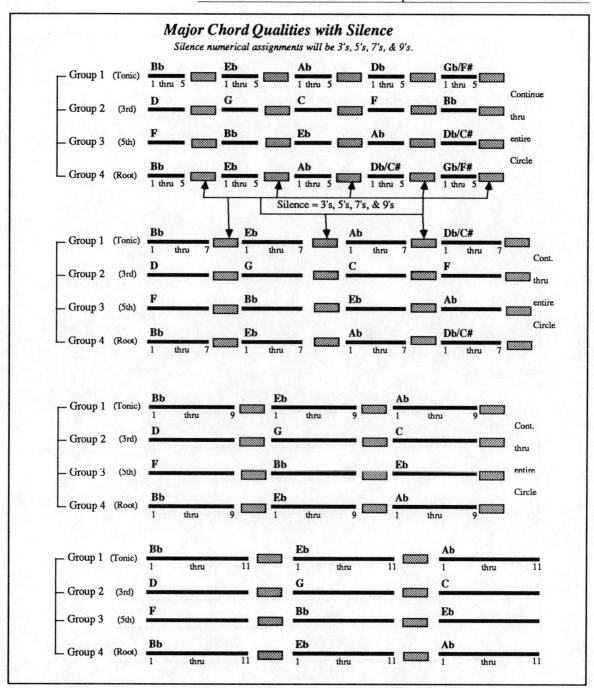

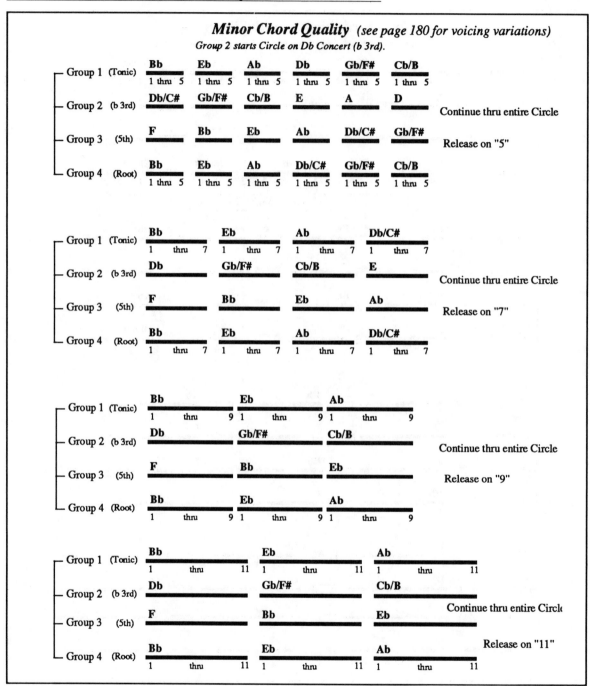

Minor Chord Quality with Silence

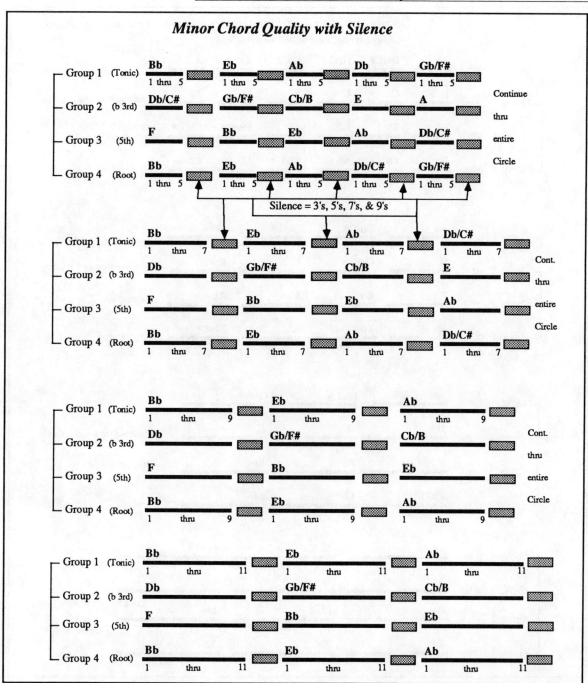

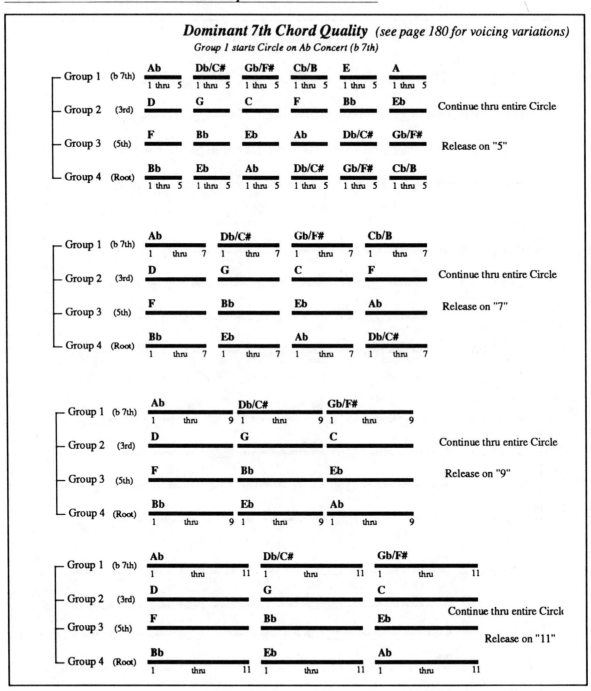

Dominant 7th Chord Quality *(see page 180 for voicing variations)*

Group 1 starts Circle on Ab Concert (b 7th)

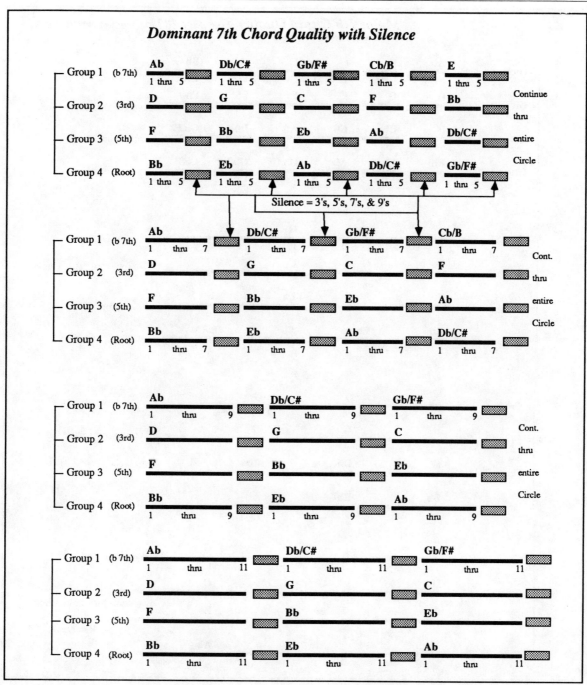

Dominant 7th Chord Quality with Silence

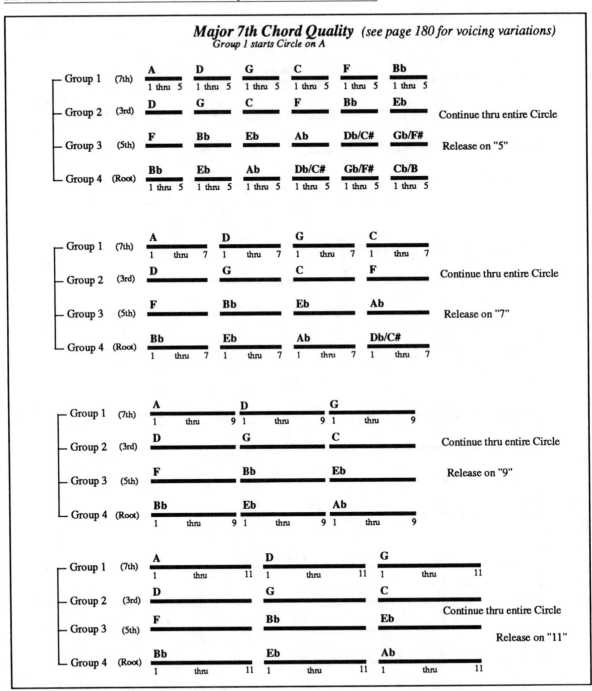

Major 7th Chord Quality *(see page 180 for voicing variations)*
Group 1 starts Circle on A

		A	D	G	C	F	Bb	
Group 1	(7th)	1 thru 5	1 thru 5	1 thru 5	1 thru 5	1 thru 5	1 thru 5	
Group 2	(3rd)	D	G	C	F	Bb	Eb	Continue thru entire Circle
Group 3	(5th)	F	Bb	Eb	Ab	Db/C#	Gb/F#	Release on "5"
Group 4	(Root)	Bb	Eb	Ab	Db/C#	Gb/F#	Cb/B	
		1 thru 5	1 thru 5	1 thru 5	1 thru 5	1 thru 5	1 thru 5	

		A	D	G	C	
Group 1	(7th)	1 thru 7	1 thru 7	1 thru 7	1 thru 7	
Group 2	(3rd)	D	G	C	F	Continue thru entire Circle
Group 3	(5th)	F	Bb	Eb	Ab	Release on "7"
Group 4	(Root)	Bb	Eb	Ab	Db/C#	
		1 thru 7	1 thru 7	1 thru 7	1 thru 7	

		A	D	G	
Group 1	(7th)	1 thru 9	1 thru 9	1 thru 9	
Group 2	(3rd)	D	G	C	Continue thru entire Circle
Group 3	(5th)	F	Bb	Eb	Release on "9"
Group 4	(Root)	Bb	Eb	Ab	
		1 thru 9	1 thru 9	1 thru 9	

		A	D	G	
Group 1	(7th)	1 thru 11	1 thru 11	1 thru 11	
Group 2	(3rd)	D	G	C	Continue thru entire Circle
Group 3	(5th)	F	Bb	Eb	Release on "11"
Group 4	(Root)	Bb	Eb	Ab	
		1 thru 11	1 thru 11	1 thru 11	

174

Major 7th Chord Quality with Silence

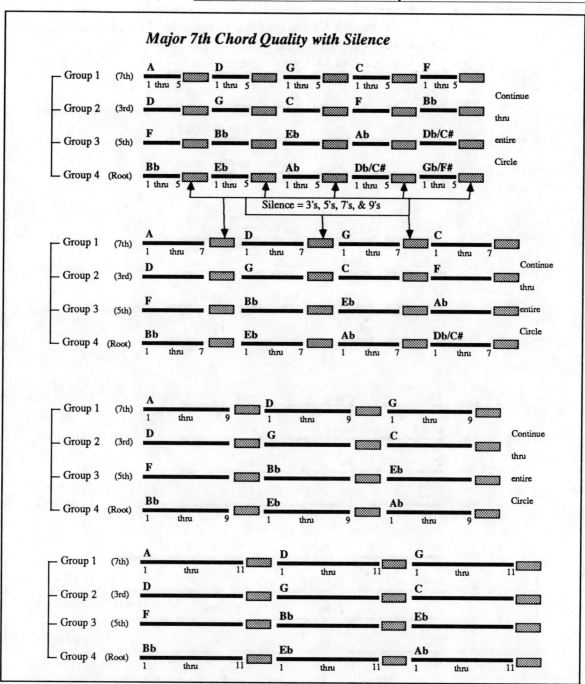

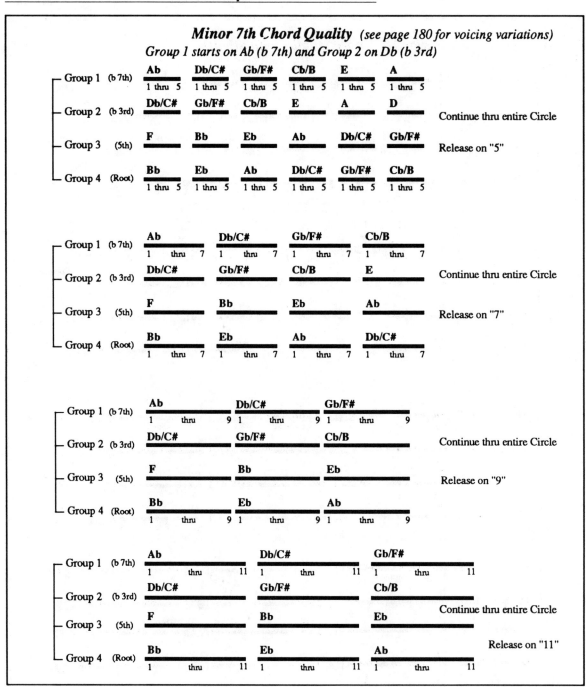

Minor 7th Chord Quality *(see page 180 for voicing variations)*

Group 1 starts on Ab (b 7th) and Group 2 on Db (b 3rd)

Group 1 (b 7th) — Ab · Db/C# · Gb/F# · Cb/B · E · A (1 thru 5)

Group 2 (b 3rd) — Db/C# · Gb/F# · Cb/B · E · A · D — Continue thru entire Circle

Group 3 (5th) — F · Bb · Eb · Ab · Db/C# · Gb/F# — Release on "5"

Group 4 (Root) — Bb · Eb · Ab · Db/C# · Gb/F# · Cb/B (1 thru 5)

Group 1 (b 7th) — Ab · Db/C# · Gb/F# · Cb/B (1 thru 7)

Group 2 (b 3rd) — Db/C# · Gb/F# · Cb/B · E — Continue thru entire Circle

Group 3 (5th) — F · Bb · Eb · Ab — Release on "7"

Group 4 (Root) — Bb · Eb · Ab · Db/C# (1 thru 7)

Group 1 (b 7th) — Ab · Db/C# · Gb/F# (1 thru 9)

Group 2 (b 3rd) — Db/C# · Gb/F# · Cb/B — Continue thru entire Circle

Group 3 (5th) — F · Bb · Eb — Release on "9"

Group 4 (Root) — Bb · Eb · Ab (1 thru 9)

Group 1 (b 7th) — Ab · Db/C# · Gb/F# (1 thru 11)

Group 2 (b 3rd) — Db/C# · Gb/F# · Cb/B

Group 3 (5th) — F · Bb · Eb — Continue thru entire Circle

Group 4 (Root) — Bb · Eb · Ab — Release on "11" (1 thru 11)

176

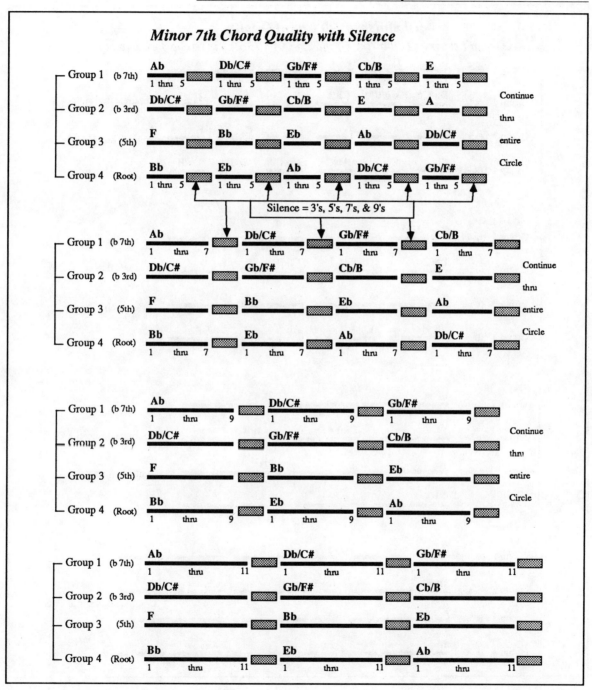

Minor 7th Chord Quality with Silence

177

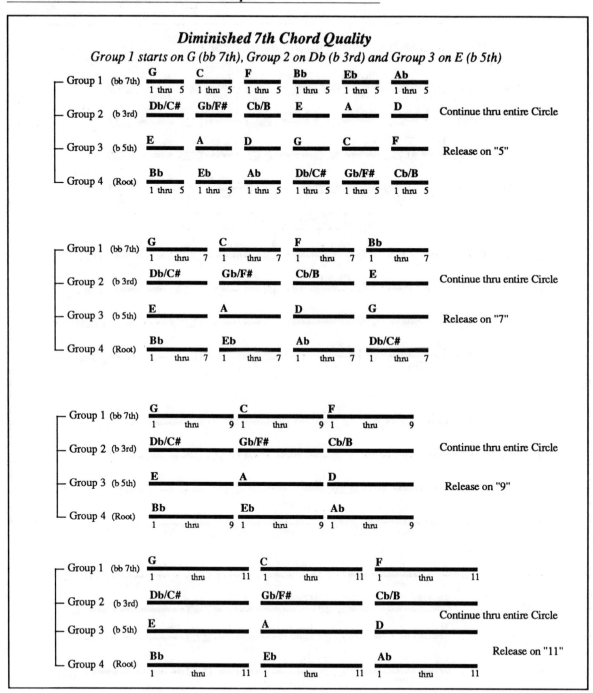

Diminished 7th Chord Quality with Silence

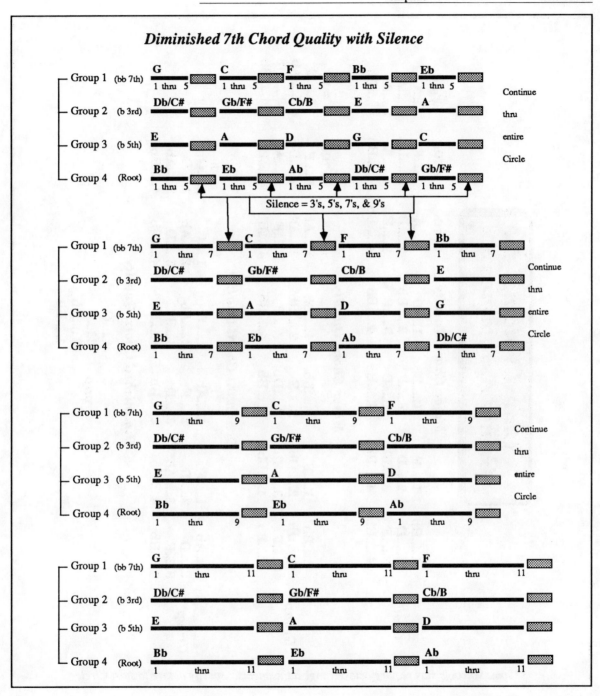

Chord Voicing Group Assignments

Major Chord Quality

Group				M 7th	M 7th*	M 9th
1....Bb	1....F	1....D		1....A	1....F	1....C
2....D	2....D	2....Bb		2....D	2....D	2....A
3....F	3....Bb	3....F		3....F	3....A	3....D
4....Bb	4....Bb	4....Bb		4....Bb	4....Bb	4....Bb

Minor Chord Quality

Group				m 7th	m 7th*	m 9th
1....Bb	1....F	1....Db		1....Ab	1....F	1....C
2....Db	2....Db	2....Bb		2....Db	2....Db	2....Ab
3....F	3....Bb	3....F		3....F	3....Ab	3....Db
4....Bb	4....Bb	4....Bb		4....Bb	4....Bb	4....Bb

Dominant Chord Quality

Group			9th	13th
1....Ab	1....F	1....D	1....C	1....G
2....D	2....D	2....Ab	2....Ab	2....D
3....F	3....Ab*	3....F	3....D	3....Ab
4....Bb	4....Bb	4....Bb	4....Bb	4....Bb

Diminished Chord Quality

Group
1....G
2....E
3....Db
4....Bb

**Some voicings may require octave/range adjustments....specify octave to start Circle

Basic Rhythm Pattern Variations

Once the students have become acquainted with processing the basic Duration Exercises and the various odd number combinations of sound and silence, proceed with the Rhythmic Exercises on the following pages. The rhythmic variations are at basic levels and should be altered to accomodate the rhythmic complexities of your selected literature.

Emphasis should be as follows:

1.   Review concepts and techniques found in Chapter 5 dealing with Rhythmic Perception *(Ruler of Time - page 182)*.

2.   Stress and emphasize Vertical and Horizontal Sound Structure *(clarity and definition of rhythm patterns is determined by the unified internal pulse of the mental process)*.

3.   Once you have established the pulse or beat, step away from the podum and listen carefully for *Internal Ensemble Pulse*.

****

181

Ruler of Time

This graphic design allows the student to create a visual awareness to the 'exactness or perfection' of their rhythmic response. The student is able to first SEE, and then LISTEN. This provides an additional sensory response and significantly improves the listening skill.

The measurement of this "space" and its sub-divisions must be mentally synchronized within the entire ensemble for rhythmic accuracy and clarity. This mental unification (and awareness) of internal pulse should be the highest priority with the instruction of rhythms !

The *length* and *width* of the *Ruler of Time* is determined by *tempo*.
"The total span of time consumed by all the events in a measure cannot exceed the duration of that measure."
   Frank R. Wilson, M.D. Clinical Professor, Dept. of Neurology, Univ. of California School of Medicine, San Francisco

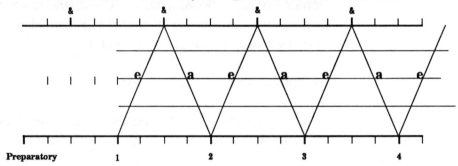

1. The lower and upper horizontal lines represent the 'down and up' beat of the conductors baton.
2. The 3 horizontal lines between the down and up beat represent 16th & 32nd note sub-divisions.
*****The *slower* the tempo, the *longer* and *wider* 'space' of sub-divisions.
*****The *faster* the tempo, the *shorter* and *narrower* 'space' of sub-divisions.

Graphic representing 4 quarter notes played with precise spacing

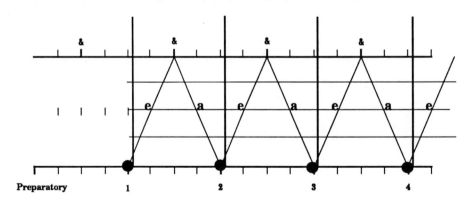

Basic Rhythm Patterns with Silence

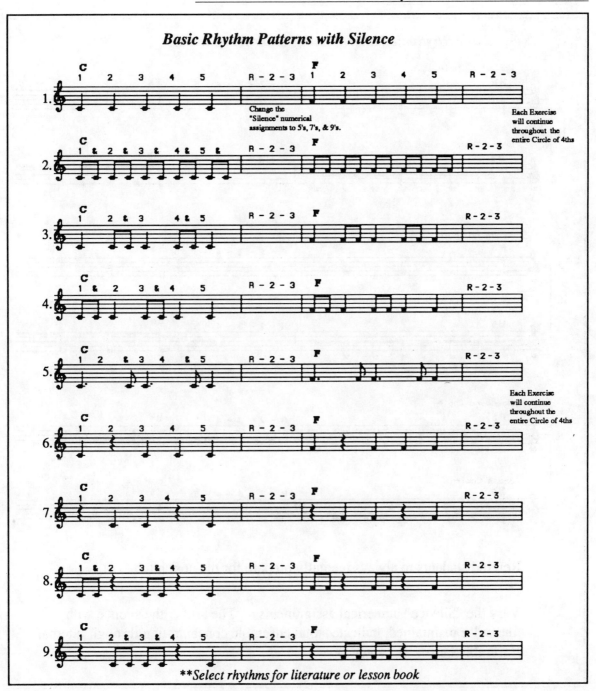

**Select rhythms for literature or lesson book

Basic Rhythmic Patterns using Choir Assignments

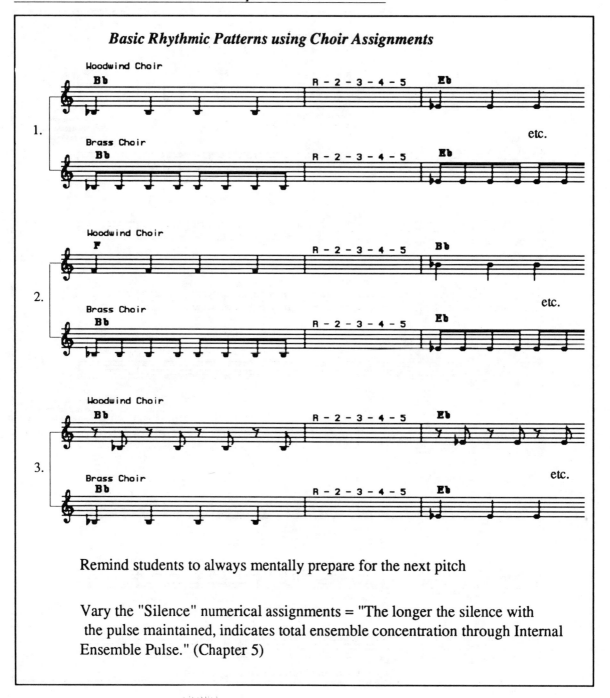

Remind students to always mentally prepare for the next pitch

Vary the "Silence" numerical assignments = "The longer the silence with the pulse maintained, indicates total ensemble concentration through Internal Ensemble Pulse." (Chapter 5)

Intermediate to Advanced Levels

Variations are to be expanded to include Chord Quality Group Assignments, Mixed Meter.

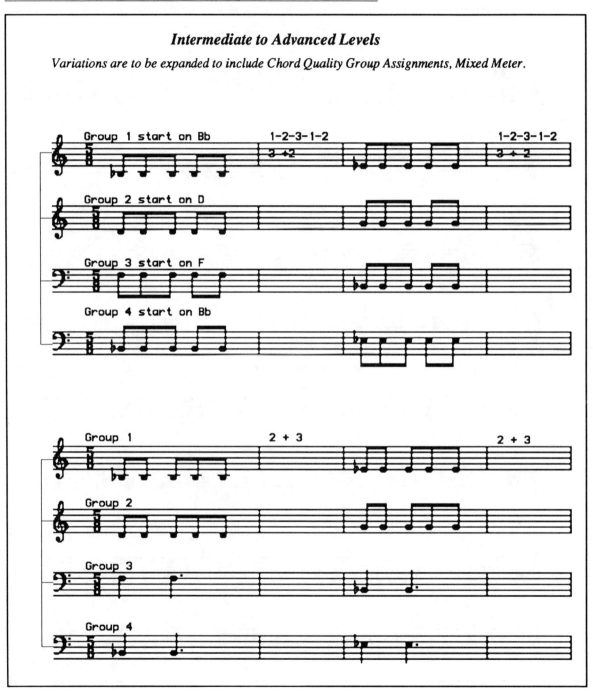

Standard Exercises without Silence - 4/4

In addition to Unisons and Octaves, use Chord Quality Group Assignments (Refer to Chapter 2)

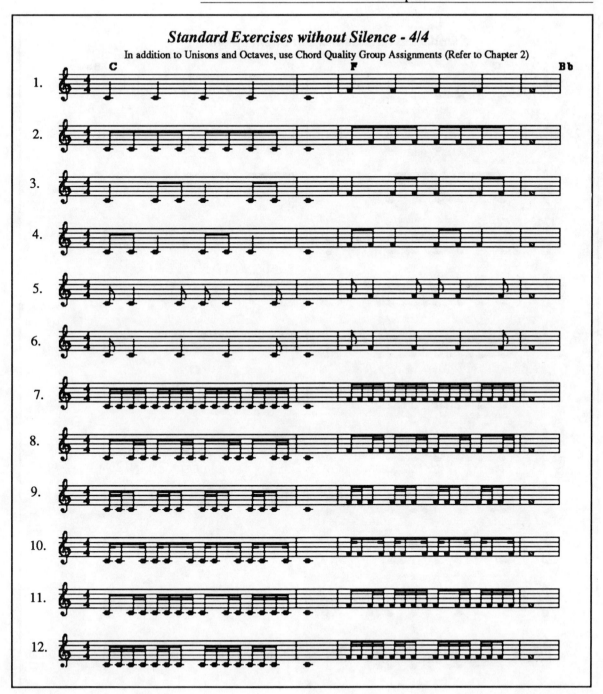

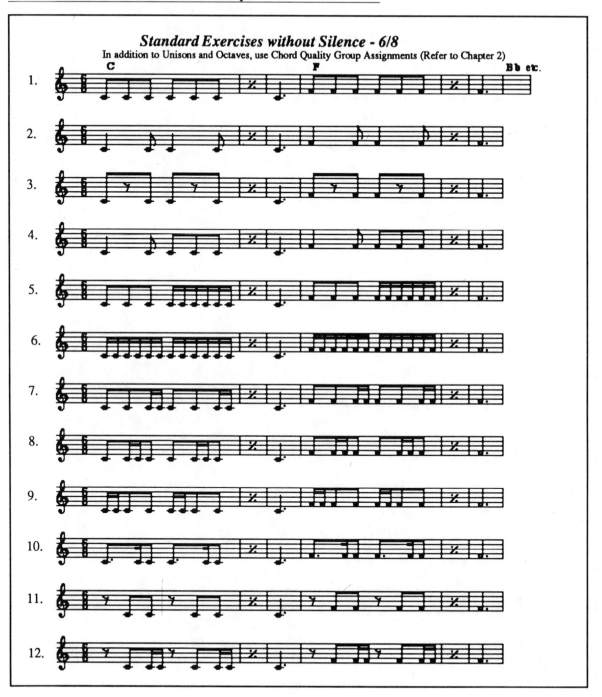

Dynamics #1

(Refer to Chapter 6)

> *Numbers imply values.*
>
> *The larger number indicates greater volume.*
>
> *The smaller number indicates less volume.*
>
> *Students respond to volume levels as they mentally process the numbers while playing.*

Ex. #1
5 - 4 - 3 - 2 - 1
F ⟶ P

Ex. #2
7 - 6 - 5 - 4 - 3 - 2 - 1
FF ⟶ P

Ex. #3
9 - 8 - 7 - 6 - 5 - 4 - 3 - 2 - 1
FF ⟶ PP

> *When introducing Dynamics, the following sequence is important:*
> 1. *Decrescendo*
> 2. *Crescendo*
> 3. *Combine Decrescendo - Crescendo*
> 4. *Any type of variation*

Ex. #4
11 - 10 - 9 - 8 - 7 - 6 - 5 - 4 - 3 - 2 - 1
FFF ⟶ PP

Dynamics #2

> *Instructional Priorities:*
>
> 1. *Tempo Variation*
> 2. *Visualize*
>   a. *Horizontal Sound Structure*
>   b. *Vertical Sound Structure*
>   c. *Color/Quality of Sound*

Ex. #5
1 - 2 - 3 - 4 - 5
P ⟶ F

Ex. #6
1 - 2 - 3 - 4 - 5 - 6 - 7
P ⟶ FF

Ex. #7
1 - 2 - 3 - 4 - 5 - 6 - 7 - 8 - 9
PP ⟶ FF

> *The performance demand increases as the duration of the Crescendo/Decrescendo increases !*

Ex. #8
1 - 2 - 3 - 4 - 5 - 6 - 7 - 8 - 9 - 10 - 11
PP ⟶ FFF

Dynamics #2

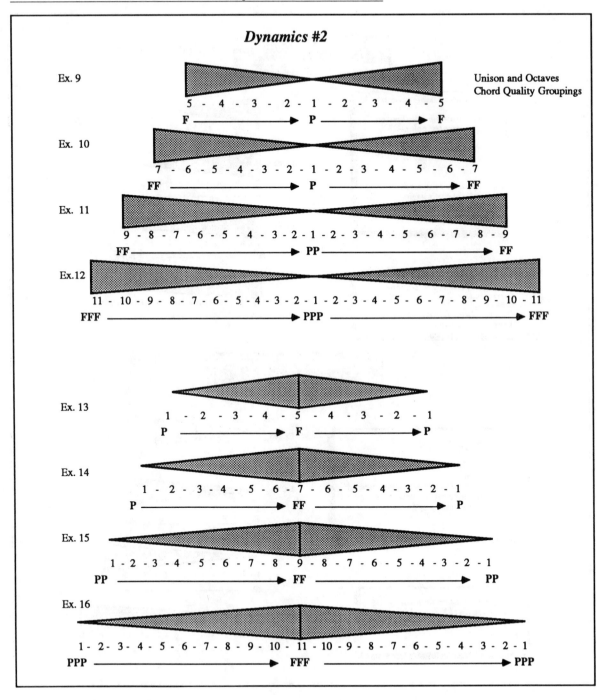

Ex. 9

Unison and Octaves
Chord Quality Groupings

5 - 4 - 3 - 2 - 1 - 2 - 3 - 4 - 5

F ⟶ P ⟶ F

Ex. 10

7 - 6 - 5 - 4 - 3 - 2 - 1 - 2 - 3 - 4 - 5 - 6 - 7

FF ⟶ P ⟶ FF

Ex. 11

9 - 8 - 7 - 6 - 5 - 4 - 3 - 2 - 1 - 2 - 3 - 4 - 5 - 6 - 7 - 8 - 9

FF ⟶ PP ⟶ FF

Ex.12

11 - 10 - 9 - 8 - 7 - 6 - 5 - 4 - 3 - 2 - 1 - 2 - 3 - 4 - 5 - 6 - 7 - 8 - 9 - 10 - 11

FFF ⟶ PPP ⟶ FFF

Ex. 13

1 - 2 - 3 - 4 - 5 - 4 - 3 - 2 - 1

P ⟶ F ⟶ P

Ex. 14

1 - 2 - 3 - 4 - 5 - 6 - 7 - 6 - 5 - 4 - 3 - 2 - 1

P ⟶ FF ⟶ P

Ex. 15

1 - 2 - 3 - 4 - 5 - 6 - 7 - 8 - 9 - 8 - 7 - 6 - 5 - 4 - 3 - 2 - 1

PP ⟶ FF ⟶ PP

Ex. 16

1 - 2 - 3 - 4 - 5 - 6 - 7 - 8 - 9 - 10 - 11 - 10 - 9 - 8 - 7 - 6 - 5 - 4 - 3 - 2 - 1

PPP ⟶ FFF ⟶ PPP

190

Dynamics #3
Full Ensemble with Silence Variations - Use all Chord Quality Groupings (Chapter 2)
(Place emphasis toward Entrance and Release = Horizontal and Vertical Sound Structure)

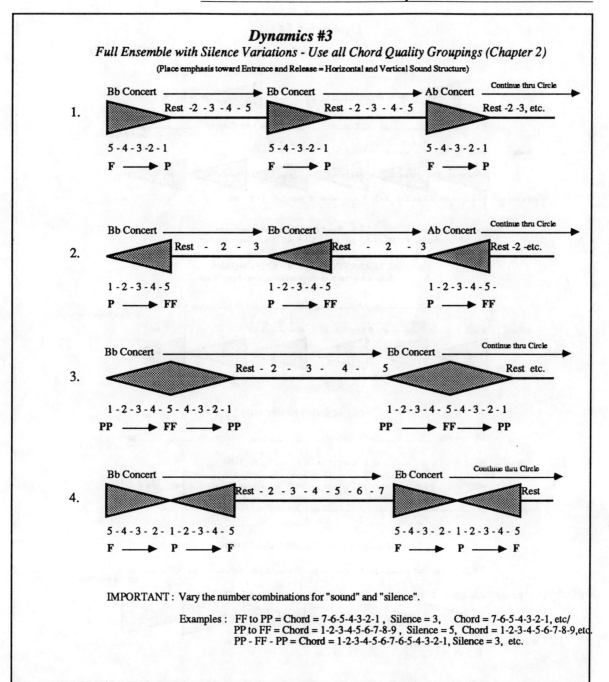

IMPORTANT : Vary the number combinations for "sound" and "silence".

Examples : FF to PP = Chord = 7-6-5-4-3-2-1 , Silence = 3,   Chord = 7-6-5-4-3-2-1, etc/
            PP to FF = Chord = 1-2-3-4-5-6-7-8-9 , Silence = 5, Chord = 1-2-3-4-5-6-7-8-9,etc.
            PP - FF - PP = Chord = 1-2-3-4-5-6-7-6-5-4-3-2-1, Silence = 3, etc.

Dynamics #4

Alternating Choirs with Decrescenco - Use all Chord Quality Groupings (Chapter 2)

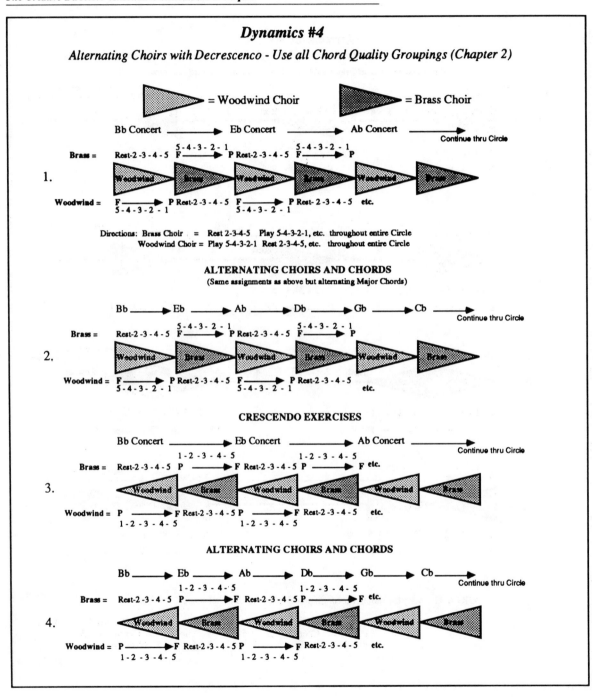

= Woodwind Choir   = Brass Choir

1.

Bb Concert ⟶ Eb Concert ⟶ Ab Concert ⟶ Continue thru Circle

Brass = Rest-2 -3 - 4 - 5   F ⟶ P   Rest-2 -3 - 4 - 5   F ⟶ P
                             5 - 4 - 3 - 2 - 1   5 - 4 - 3 - 2 - 1

Woodwind = F ⟶ P   Rest-2 -3 - 4 - 5   F ⟶ P   Rest-2 -3 - 4 - 5   etc.
            5 - 4 - 3 - 2 - 1   5 - 4 - 3 - 2 - 1

Directions: Brass Choir = Rest 2-3-4-5   Play 5-4-3-2-1, etc. throughout entire Circle
Woodwind Choir = Play 5-4-3-2-1   Rest 2-3-4-5, etc.   throughout entire Circle

ALTERNATING CHOIRS AND CHORDS
(Same assignments as above but alternating Major Chords)

2.

Bb ⟶ Eb ⟶ Ab ⟶ Db ⟶ Gb ⟶ Cb ⟶ Continue thru Circle

Brass = Rest-2 -3 - 4 - 5   F ⟶ P   Rest-2 -3 - 4 - 5   F ⟶ P
                             5 - 4 - 3 - 2 - 1   5 - 4 - 3 - 2 - 1

Woodwind = F ⟶ P   Rest-2 -3 - 4 - 5   F ⟶ P   Rest-2 -3 - 4 - 5
            5 - 4 - 3 - 2 - 1   5 - 4 - 3 - 2 - 1   etc.

CRESCENDO EXERCISES

3.

Bb Concert ⟶ Eb Concert ⟶ Ab Concert ⟶ Continue thru Circle

Brass = Rest-2 -3 - 4 - 5   P ⟶ F   Rest-2 -3 - 4 - 5   P ⟶ F   etc.
                             1 - 2 - 3 - 4 - 5   1 - 2 - 3 - 4 - 5

Woodwind = P ⟶ F   Rest-2 -3 - 4 - 5   P ⟶ F   Rest-2 -3 - 4 - 5   etc.
            1 - 2 - 3 - 4 - 5   1 - 2 - 3 - 4 - 5

ALTERNATING CHOIRS AND CHORDS

4.

Bb ⟶ Eb ⟶ Ab ⟶ Db ⟶ Gb ⟶ Cb ⟶ Continue thru Circle

Brass = Rest-2 -3 - 4 - 5   P ⟶ F   Rest-2 -3 - 4 - 5 P ⟶ F   etc.
                             1 - 2 - 3 - 4 - 5   1 - 2 - 3 - 4 - 5

Woodwind = P ⟶ F   Rest-2 -3 - 4 - 5 P ⟶ F   Rest-2 -3 - 4 - 5   etc.
            1 - 2 - 3 - 4 - 5   1 - 2 - 3 - 4 - 5

Dynamics #5

Alternating Choirs with Silence - Use all Chord Quality Groupings (Chapter 2)

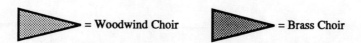

= Woodwind Choir   = Brass Choir

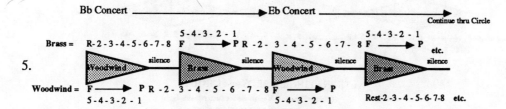

Bb Concert ————————————→ Eb Concert ————————————→
Continue thru Circle

Brass = R-2-3-4-5-6-7-8 F 5-4-3-2-1 → P R-2-3-4-5-6-7-8 F 5-4-3-2-1 → P etc.

5.   Woodwind   silence   Brass   silence   Woodwind   silence   Brass   silence

Woodwind = F → P 5-4-3-2-1 R-2-3-4-5-6-7-8 F → P 5-4-3-2-1 Rest-2-3-4-5-6-7-8 etc.

Directions: Brass Choir = Rest 2,3,4,5,6,7,8 - Play 5-4-3-2-1-Rest 2,3,4,5,6,7,8 etc. thru entire Circle
Woodwind Choir = Play 5-4-3-2-1 Rest 2,3,4,5,6,7,8, Play 5-4-3-2-1 etc. thru entire Circle

ALTERNATING CHORDS

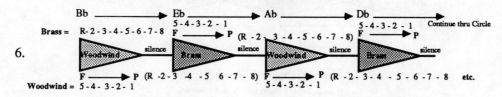

Bb ————→ Eb ————→ Ab ————→ Db ————→
Continue thru Circle

Brass = R-2-3-4-5-6-7-8 F 5-4-3-2-1 → P (R-2 3-4-5-6-7-8) F 5-4-3-2-1 → P

6.   Woodwind   silence   Brass   silence   Woodwind   silence   Brass   silence

Woodwind = F → P 5-4-3-2-1 (R-2-3-4-5 6-7-8) F → P 5-4-3-2-1 (R-2-3-4-5-6-7-8) etc.

CRESCENDO EXERCISES and "Silence"

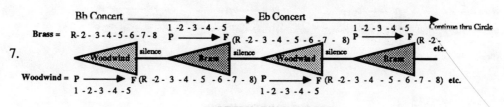

Bb Concert ————————————→ Eb Concert ————————————→
Continue thru Circle

Brass = R-2-3-4-5-6-7-8 P 1-2-3-4-5 → F (R-2-3-4-5-6-7-8) P 1-2-3-4-5 → F (R-2- etc.

7.   Woodwind   silence   Brass   silence   Woodwind   silence   Brass

Woodwind = P → F 1-2-3-4-5 (R-2-3-4-5-6-7-8) P → F 1-2-3-4-5 (R-2-3-4-5-6-7-8) etc.

ALTERNATING CHORDS

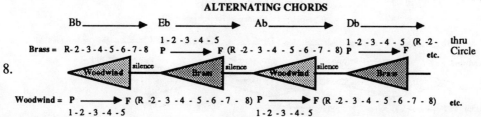

Bb ————→ Eb ————→ Ab ————→ Db ————→

Brass = R-2-3-4-5-6-7-8 P 1-2-3-4-5 → F (R-2-3-4-5-6-7-8) P 1-2-3-4-5 → F (R-2- thru Circle etc.

8.   Woodwind   silence   Brass   silence   Woodwind   silence   Brass

Woodwind = P → F 1-2-3-4-5 (R-2-3-4-5-6-7-8) P → F 1-2-3-4-5 (R-2-3-4-5-6-7-8) etc.

Dynamics #6
Use all Chord Quality Groupings (Chapter 2)

ALTERNATING CHOIRS AND DYNAMICS
(Change Dynamic Variations for each rehearsal)

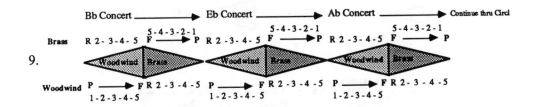

ALTERNATING CHORDS and CHOIRS
(Change Dynamic Variations for each rehearsal)
Same numerical assignments as above

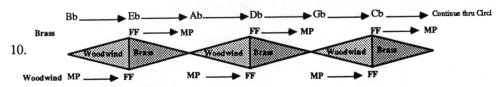

Number combinations should vary with 7's, 9's and 11's

REVERSING CHOIRS and DYNAMICS
(Change Dynamic Variations for each rehearsal)

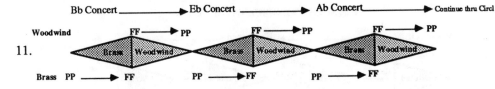

ALTERNATE CHORDS
(Change Dynamic Variations for each rehearsal)

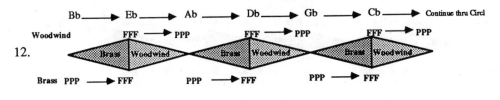

Dynamics #7
Use all Chord Quality Groupings (Chapter 2)
ALTERNATING CHOIRS, DYNAMICS and "SILENCE"

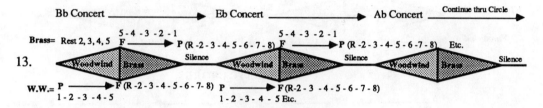

ALTERNATE CHORDS
(Same numerical assignments)

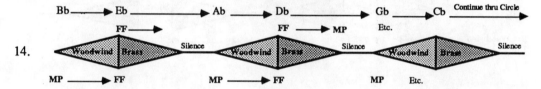

REVERSE CHOIRS and DYNAMICS

(Use same Number Assignments as above exercises)

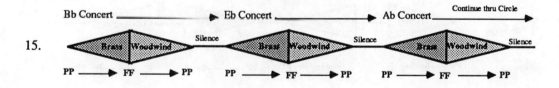

ALTERNATE CHORDS

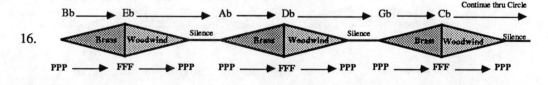

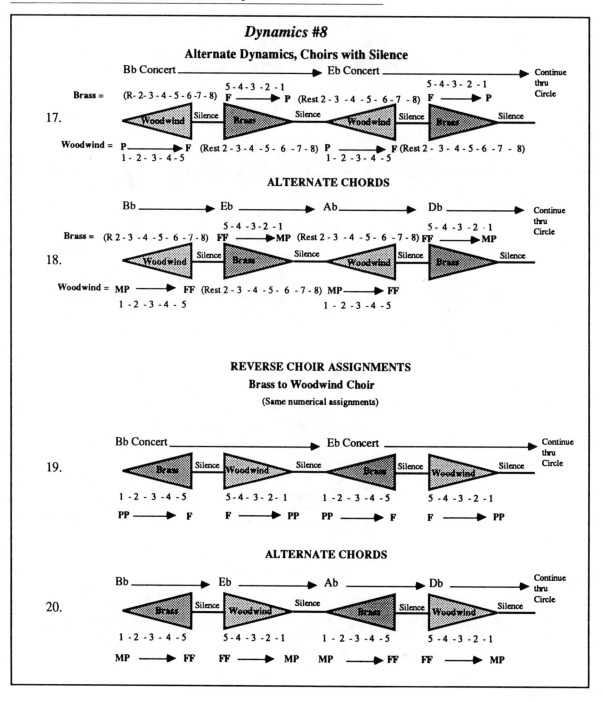

Dynamics #8

Alternate Dynamics, Choirs with Silence

ALTERNATE CHORDS

REVERSE CHOIR ASSIGNMENTS
Brass to Woodwind Choir
(Same numerical assignments)

ALTERNATE CHORDS

Dynamics #9
Percy Grainger Color "Shifts" (very effective for Grainger literature)
Use all Chord Quality Groupings (Chapter 2)

Woodwind Choir plays PP-F-PP   Brass Choir plays F-PP-F

Both Choirs play their Dynamic Assignment simultaneously to create "Color Shifts"

Bb Concert ⟶ Eb Concert ⟶ Ab Concert

F ⟶ PP ⟶ F   F ⟶ PP ⟶ F   Continue thru Circle

21.

Brass Choir = 5 - 4 - 3 - 2 - 1 - 2 - 3 - 4 - 5   5 - 4 - 3 - 2 - 1 - 2 - 3 - 4 - 5   R-2-3

Woodwind Choir = 1 - 2 - 3 - 4 - 5 - 4 - 3 - 2 - 1   1 - 2 - 3 - 4 - 5 - 4 - 3 - 2 - 1   R-2-3

PP ⟶ F ⟶ PP   PP ⟶ F ⟶ PP

Reverse Dynamic Assignments from the above exercise.

Bb Concert ⟶ Eb Concert ⟶ Ab Concert

PP ⟶ F ⟶ PP   PP ⟶ F ⟶ PP   Continue thru Circle

22.

Brass Choir = 1 - 2 - 3 - 4 - 5 - 4 - 3 - 2 - 1   1 - 2 - 3 - 4 - 5 - 4 - 3 - 2 - 1   R-2-3

Woodwind Choir = 5 - 4 - 3 - 2 - 1 - 2 - 3 - 4 - 5   5 - 4 - 3 - 2 - 1 - 2 - 3 - 4 - 5   R-2-3

F ⟶ PP ⟶ F   F ⟶ PP ⟶ F

F ⟶ PP ⟶ F   F ⟶ PP ⟶ F

23.

Brass Choir = 7 - 6 -5 -4 -3 -2 -1 -2 -3 - 4 -5 - 6 -7 (R-2-3) 7 - 6 -5 -4 -3 -2 -1 -2 -3 - 4 -5 - 6 -7 (R-2-3)

Woodwind Choir = (R- 2 - 3) 1- 2- 3- 4- 5- 6- 7- 6- 5- 4- 3- 2 -1 (R- 2 -3) 1- 2- 3- 4- 5- 6- 7- 6- 5- 4- 3- 2 -1

PP ⟶ F ⟶ PP   PP ⟶ F ⟶ PP

F ⟶ PP ⟶ F   F ⟶ PP ⟶ F

24.

Brass Choir = 7 - 6 -5 -4 -3 -2 -1 -2 -3 - 4 -5 - 6 -7 (R-2-3) 7 - 6 -5 -4 -3 -2 -1 -2 -3 - 4 -5 - 6 -7 (R-2-3)

Woodwind Choir = (R- 2 - 3) 1- 2- 3- 4- 5- 6- 7- 6- 5- 4- 3- 2 -1 (R- 2 -3) 1- 2- 3- 4- 5- 6- 7- 6- 5- 4- 3- 2 -1

PP ⟶ F ⟶ PP   PP ⟶ F ⟶ PP

197

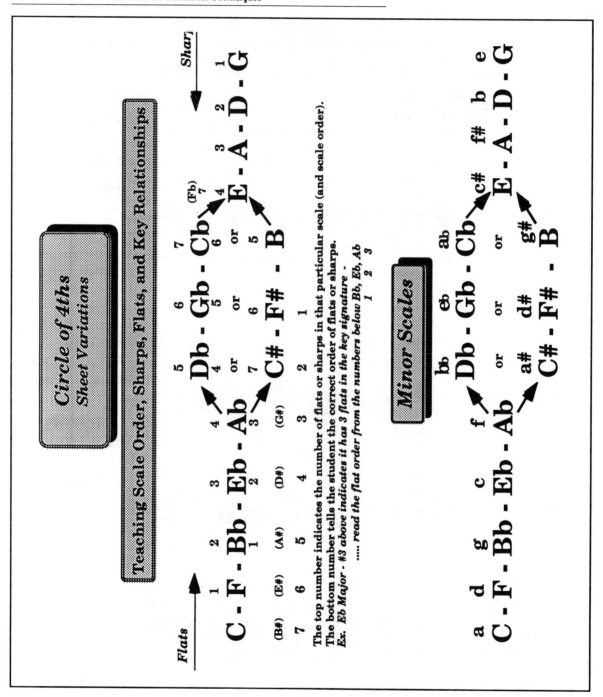

Scale Variations
Play each example throughout the entire Circle of 4ths (Chapter 2)
*Asterisk indicates where students specifically think and prepare for the next key

Scale Variations (Cont.)

All scale examples can be played with the above variations

Alternating Ascending and Descending Scales

* Apply Choir and Chord Quality Group Assignments for the above Scale Variations.

Alternating Ascending and Descending Scales (Cont.)

* Vary Articulation patterns for all Scale Variations.

Alternating Ascending and Descending Scales (Cont.)

* When your ensemble is able to perform the above Scale Variations, they will be functioning in an advanced level of mental processing and technical facility.

* Variations for the above exercises are done through articulation patterns along with Choir and Chord Quality Group Assignments.

Chromatic Scale Variations with Circle of 4ths

Chromatic Scales are to include:

1. Choir Assignments (intervals of the 3rds, 5ths, 6ths)
   a. 3rds = Brass start Bb - Woodwinds start on D concert
   b. 5ths = Brass start Bb - Woodwinds start on F concert
   c. 6ths = Brass start Bb - Woodwinds start on G concert

2. Chord Quality Group Assignments (major, minor, etc.)

Digital Patterns
Compressing Key Tonality (Chapter 2)

Digital Patterns (Cont.)

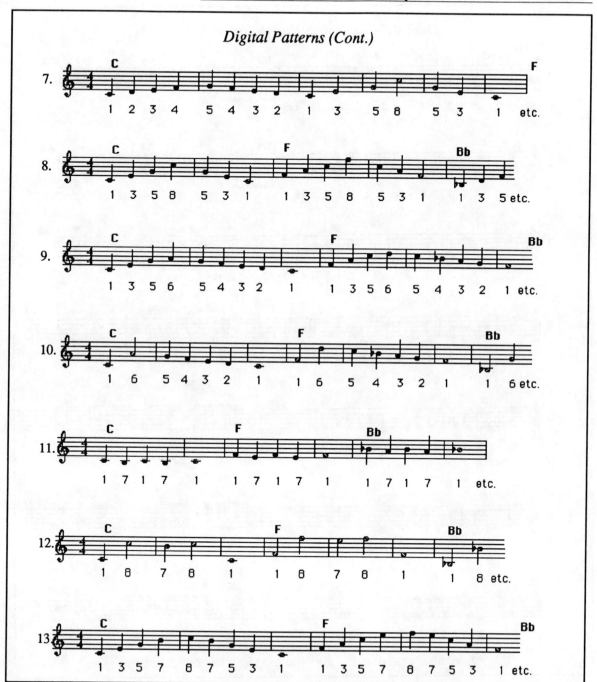

Digital Patterns with Eighth Notes

* Mentally prepare or "fix" the next key in your mind !

Digital Patterns with Eighth Notes (Cont.)

Digital Patterns with Sixteenth Notes

Digital Patterns with Sixteenths (Cont.)

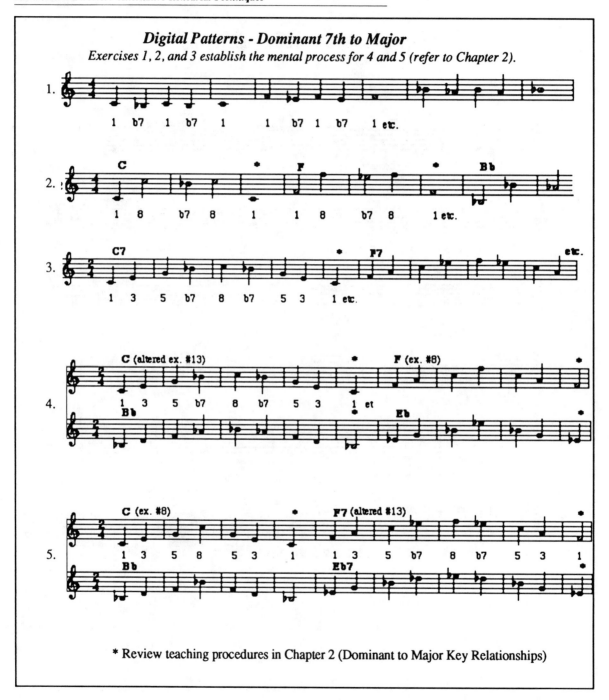

Digital Patterns - Dominant 7th to Major
Exercises 1, 2, and 3 establish the mental process for 4 and 5 (refer to Chapter 2).

* Review teaching procedures in Chapter 2 (Dominant to Major Key Relationships)

Pyramids of Auditory Skills

OPTIMUM
PERFORMANCE
QUALITY !!!

Integrated Elements

Individual → Pyramid of Auditory Skills #1 ← Section

Total Ensemble

Integrated Elements

Balance-Blend → Pyramid of Auditory Skills #2 ← Intonation

Tone Quality

Integrated Elements

Vertical Sound Structure → Pyramid of Auditory Skills #3 ← Color Timbre

Horizontal Sound Structure

Foundation of Band Performance Quality

Knowledge Experience → #4 Conductor ← Teaching Techniques

LISTENING SKILLS

Superior Performance Tetrahedron

PYRAMID 4 serves as the foundation and determines the process to the pinnacle of *OPTIMUM PERFORMANCE QUALITY!* This performance quality is determined by the instructional techniques and wholistic concepts necessary to integrate all elements in PYRAMIDS 1, 2, and 3.

213

Listening
(Balance, Blend, Intonation)

3 Logical Steps to Balance, Blend, Intonation

1. **If you hear yourself above all others (section/band) :**
   You are overpowering or overblowing !
   Make the necessary adjustment - remove your "identity."
   This initiates an *auditory reaction to BALANCE.*

2. **If you still hear yourself and you made the adjustment in #1, then:**
   You are playing with poor TONE QUALITY !
   Make the necessary adjustment....embouchure, breath support, posture, equipment.
   This initiates a physical reaction to embouchure, breath support and posture
   and an *auditory reaction to BLEND* (Poor Tone Quality will not blend with anything).

3. **If you still hear yourself and you made the adjustment in #2, then:**
   You are playing out of tune ! Make the necessary adjustment. Lengthen or
   shorten your instrument (continue with 6 step "Beatless Tuning" Sequence)
   This initiates an *auditory reaction to "Beatless Tuning."*

**The above steps are prioritized. The relationships of these 3 steps are extremely important. One cannot come before the other. *An instrument cannot be played in tune if overblowing or poor tone quality exists.* Instruct your students to follow this logical process if improved ensemble sound is expected. When 2 or more students play the same pitch in perfect balance, blend, and in tune....*their "identity" is removed..... they effectively contribute to the excellence of ensemble tone quality and become a part of the "whole."*

(Duplicate for students)

214

Listening
(Intonation)

Logical Steps to Effective Intonation
"Beatless Tuning"

It is not important to recognize sharpness or flatness, *only speed of the beats.*
Principal Player of each section is responsible for the intonation of the section.
Principal Player plays tuning pitch.
1. Player #2 plays pitch and only listens for the "beats" for out of tuneness.
    Instruct player to make any adjustment with barrel, mouthpiece or slide.
    Listen for the "beats", did they speed up or slow down ? (student is not to answer
    this question - student will determine and respond accordingly to the next step.

2. If the "beats" were **faster**.....
    .....*you made the wrong move, adjust the instrument in the opposite direction.*

3. If the "beats" became **slower**.....
    .....*you are making the correct move, continue until all "beats" are eliminated.*

4. If you find yourself **"pinching"** your embouchure to eliminate "beats".....
    .....*your horn is too long, it must be shortened.*

5. If you find yourself **"relaxing"** your embouchure to eliminate "beats".....
    .....*your instrument is too short, it must be lengthened.*

6. When 2 or more similar pitches are played and the sound is "beatless" (and not
    using any pressure or relaxation)....*YOU ARE PERFECTLY IN TUNE !*

(Duplicate for students)

215

Suggestions & Reminders

1. Rehearsal structure..... *change your day to day habits !* The first 10 minutes is extremely important for effective learning.... all warm-up musical demands (intonation, balance, blend, articulation, rhythms, etc.) should be *LINKED to the literature to be rehearsed.*

2. Make a gradual transition from your regular rehearsal pattern to *Alternative Rehearsal Techniques.* The concepts and instructional procedures are designed to *enhance your present techniques !*

3. Change and use many variations as soon as an error is made.... *don't repeat the same exercise. It is not the repetition of the exercise that is the priority.. it is the quality of the "mental signal" that determines the quality of the exercise. Musical excellence will always follow and improve at the rate of the students ability to focus concentration.*

4. *Activate....Sustain....and Control student concentration* through: Circle of 4ths variations.... unison/ octaves....chords....scales....sound & silence....rhtyhmic exercises....dynamics....articulation....digital patterns. *Students should NOT be required to memorize Circle of 4ths sheet...it is required to be on their stand during warm-up.*

5. Focus your attention to the students mental awareness and intensity of concentration.... how long are you able to control the quality of this concentration ? This happens quickly once "old habits" are removed. *The priority is to unify and synchronize thinking to produce the expected musical quality.*

6. Create *effective listening skills through visualization and imagery.... alerts a totally different sense of listening.* Always refer to sound through Horizontal and Vertical Sound Structure, Color, entrance, start of silence, etc.

7. Develop and establish an *Internal Ensemble Pulse* through odd numbers.... Synchronize and unify "thinking in time".....start conducting and step away... *don't BEAT time !*

8. Measurement of Sound and Silence... *the longer the interval of silence, with the most precise entrance, is the result of an organization that has unified their internal feeling of pulse....* the highest numbers of silence are the most demanding for concentration and should not be introduced too early.

9. To establish the *"discipline of silence"* always wait for total silence in the room... no room noises, stands moving, whispering, bells ringing, etc.

10. Increase the *"Power of Concentration"* by having *students close their eyes and visualize the sound and qualities you are stressing.* Closing eyes assures you of no wandering minds or daydreaming !! Clap your hands to alert students to open eyes.

Suggestions & Reminders (cont.)

11. The effectiveness of *Alternative Rehearsal Techniques* can be increased if presented in small group settings.

12. Refrain from writing musical examples.... be explicit with your directions and allow students to visualize and image the example or exercise. This is the process necessary to re-focus students thinking and concentration to listening rather than the mechanical needs of rhythms etc. Rhythm patterns may be notated on blackboard without pitch notation.

13. Do not revert to Bb and Eb concert... create comfort and knowledge of all keys.

14. When performing scales and scale variations, don't raise the students level of "anxiety" by having them play for the entire band. *Move throughout the band and stop and listen to sections and individuals.*

15. *Apply major literature demands to warm-up process and proceed through all keys by using the Circle of 4ths sheet.*

16. Odd number combinations.... *change number combinations at the first "break down"* ....remember you are developing controlled concentration and not habits !!

17. Sense your students power of concentration.... *unify the energy and power that is seated before you !!!!!*

Expect the following student reactions

1. You will experience some hesitancy and uneasiness when applying these techniques. This is normal until you acquaint yourself with the unlimited variations. Don't measure your capabilities to a "formula" or "recipe".... *trust the process of growth rather than the "formula."* The majority of your students will respond with a positive reaction.

2. *The "non-thinkers" will get frustrated because they have never been expected to think in this manner... be patient.*

3. Expect questions.... the students no longer have the "security" of the printed page. They must rely upon their understanding of your description.

4. You will experience some "giggling" in the early stages, especially when students close their eyes and use visualization and imagery.

The above are only temporary and will no longer exist after the second rehearsal ! Once the basic concepts are introduced, your procedures continue to unfold and expand relative to your musical expectations.

This system will allow your band to achieve levels that once seemed impossible !

Finale

*I sincerely hope you have experienced
many new insights through this
alternative system of musical learning
and
what we can do with student musicians
in our day to day instructional process.*

✳✳✳✳✳

*It is not the score or numerical grade
that makes the difference.....
it's the mysterious nature of humans
searching for expression
through non-verbal sound.*

✳✳✳✳✳

*The uniqueness of artistic expression,
coupled with differences in learning,
attitude and dedication,
is what we continue
to elevate
to form the "one being"
in this expression through
BAND !*

Suggested Readings

AESTHETICS: Dimensions For Music Education.....Abraham A. Schwadron
    Music Educators National Conference Publication (1967)
ARTS, EDUCATION & BRAIN RESEARCH.....Dr. Thomas A. Regelski
    Music Educators National Conference Publication (1978)
ART, MIND, BRAIN: A Cognitive Approach to Creativity.....Howard Gardner
    Basic Books, Inc./Harper Colophon Books (1982)
THE ART OF BEING HUMAN.....Richard P. Janaro & Thelma C. Altshuler
    Harper & Row, Publishers (1984)
THE ART OF CONDUCTING....Donald Hunsberger & Roy Ernst
    Alfred A. Knopf, Inc. (1983)
A SOPRANO ON HER HEAD.....Eloise Ristad
    Real People Press, Box F, Moab, Utah 84532 (1982)
THE BRAIN.........Richard M. Restak, M.D. (from Television Series)
    Bantam Books (1984)
BRASS WIND ARTISTRY: Master your Mind, Master Your Instrument.....Severson & McDunn
    Accura Music, Athens, Ohio (1983)
COGNITION and CURRICULUM: A Basis for Deciding What to Teach...Elliot Eisner
    Longman Publishing Co. (1982)
COMING TO OUR SENSES: The Arts, Education & American Panel
    McGraw-Hill Book Co. (1977)
DIMENSIONS OF MUSICAL THINKING....edited by Eunice Boardman
    Music Educators National Conference (1989)
THE DRAGONS OF EDEN: Speculations on the Evolution of Human Intelligence.....Carl Sagan
    Ballantine Books, Pub. (1977)
DRAWING ON THE ARTIST WITHIN.....Betty Edwards
    Simon & Schuster, Inc. (1986)
EFFECTIVE PERFORMANCE OF BAND MUSIC....W. Francis McBeth
    Southern Music Publishing Co.
THE EVERYDAY GENIUS: Restoring Children's Natural Joy of Learning.....Peter Kline
    Great Ocean Publishers, Inc. (1988)
EMOTION AND MEANING IN MUSIC.....Leonard B. Meyer
    The University of Chicago Press (1956)
THE FARTHER REACHES OF HUMAN NATURE....Abraham H. Maslow
    Penguin Books (1976)
FRAMES OF MIND: Theory of Multiple Intelligences.......Howard Gardner
    Basic Books, Inc. Publishers (1983)
FUTURE OF MUSICAL EDUCATION IN AMERICA....edited by Donald J. Shetler
    Eastman School of Music Press - Rochester, NY (1984)
GUIDE TO SCORE STUDY for the Wind Band Conductor....Frank Battisti & Robert Garofalo
    Meredith Music Publications (1990)
HANDBOOK OF MUSIC PSYCHOLOGY.....Edited by Donald A. Hodges
    National Association for Music Therapy, Inc. (1980)

Suggested Readings (cont.)

INNER GAME OF MUSIC.....Barry Green
   Anchor/Doubleday Publishers (1986)
INTRODUCTION TO THE MUSICAL BRAIN.....Don C. Campbell
   Magnamusic-Baton, Inc. (1983)
LEARNING SEQUENCES IN MUSIC.....Edwin E. Gordon
   G.I.A. Publications, Inc. (1980)
LEFT BRAIN, RIGHT BRAIN......Sally Springer & George Deutsch
   W. H. Freeman & Co. (1981)
MARCHING TO DIFFERENT DRUMMERS (Learning Styles Theory).....P. Burke Guild, S. Garger
   ASCD/Association for Supervision and Curriculum Development (1985)
MULTIMIND.....Robert Ornstein
   Anchor/Doubleday Publishing (1986)
MUSICAL PERFORMANCE: LEARNING THEORY AND PEDAGOGY.....Daniel L. Kohut
   Prentice - Hall, Inc. (1985)
THE METAPHORIC MIND: A Celebration of Creative Consciousness...Robert Samples
   Addison-Wesley Publishing Co. (1976)
THE MIND.....Richard M. Restak, M.D.
   Bantam Books (1988)
THE MIND'S NEW SCIENCE, A History of the Cognitive Revolution.....Howard Gardner
   Basic Books, Inc., Publishers (1987)
THE MODERN CONDUCTOR.....Elizabeth Green
   Prentice Hall, Inc. (1969)
THE MUSICAL MIND: The cognitive psychology of music....John A. Sloboda
   Oxford Psychology Series No. 5, Oxford University Press (1985)
NEW WORLD NEW MIND.....Robert Ornstein, Paul Ehrlich
   Doubleday Publishing (1989)
OPEN MIND / WHOLE MIND: Parenting and Teaching Tomorrow's Children Today.....Bob Samples
   Jalmar Press, Rolling Hills Estates, California (1987)
PSYCHOLOGICAL FOUNDATIONS OF MUSICAL BEHAVIOR.....Rudolaf Radocy & J. David Boyle
   Charles C. Thomas Publisher (1979)
THE ROLE OF IMAGERY IN LEARNING.....Harry S. Broudy
   Getty Center for Education in the Arts (1987)
THE SECRET POWER OF MUSIC.....David Tame
   Destiny Book/Harper & Row Publishers (1984)
THE SILENT PULSE (A search for the perfect rhythm that exists in each of us).....George Leonard
   E.P. Dutton (1978), Bantam edition (1981)
THE TIME OF MUSIC.....Jonathan D. Kramer
   Schirmer Books (1988)
TONE DEAF AND ALL THUMBS.....Dr. Frank R. Wilson
   Viking Penguin Inc. (1986)
TOWARD A NEW ERA IN ARTS EDUCATION....edited by John T. Mclaughlin
   Music Educators National Conference Publication (1988)

About the Author

Edward S. Lisk has been the Director of Bands and K-12 Music Supervisor for the Oswego City School District in Oswego, New York for the past twenty one years. He is a graduate of Syracuse University School of Music with advanced studies at Ithaca School of Music, State University College at Oswego, and Syracuse University.

The Oswego High School Bands, under the direction of Mr. Lisk, hold a long distinguished performance record. Since 1973, they have performed at most of the prestigious state and national instrumental conferences, contests, and parades. During this period of time, the Oswego Bands have had the distinguished honor of being directed by many of the nations foremost conductors and composers. The *New York State Assembly* honored the accomplishments of the Oswego High School Band Program under the direction of Mr. Lisk through Legislative Resolution in 1986 and 1988.

Mr. Lisk has traveled throughout the United States as a visiting lecturer/staff at many major universities and guest conductor/clinician at regional, state, national and international conferences during the past several years. He has had several articles published in professional journals. Reactions to his clinic presentation at the *1989 Mid-West International Band Clinic* in Chicago and other notable instrumental events have been quoted by many as "the best clinic they have attended in years." In June of 1990, he toured throughout Australia presenting clinics at conferences, universities, and schools for the *Australian National Band and Orchestra Association* .

Mr. Lisk was recently inducted for membership in the distinguished *American Bandmasters Association*. He is currently the *President* of the *National Band Association*. He holds membership in the *Music Educators National Conference, New York State School Music Association, World Association for Symphonic Bands and Ensembles*, and was one of the founders of the *New York State Band Directors Association*. He is the recipient of the Phi Delta Kappa *"Area Educator of The Year"* Award (1983), the Oswego Classroom *"Teacher of The Year"* Award (1974 & 1983), the 1989 Oswego City School District *"Administrator of The Year"* award, and the National Band Association *"Citation of Excellence."*